Exploring the Links Between International Business and Poverty Reduction: A Case Study of Unilever in Indonesia

Principal Author: Jason Clay

An Oxfam GB, Novib, Unilever, and Unilever Indonesia joint research project

Contents

Tables, figures, boxes, and case studies

Tables

Figures

Boxes

Case studies

Acronyms and abbreviations

CSO	civil-society organisation
CSR	corporate social responsibility
FDI	foreign direct investment
FTE	full-time equivalent
FMCG	fast-moving consumer goods
GDP	gross domestic product
ILO	International Labour Organization
KHM	Kebutuhan Hidup Minimum ('minimum subsistence need')
IMF	International Monetary Fund
MNC	multinational company
MOU	memorandum of understanding
MT	metric ton
NGO	non-government organisation
Rp	rupiah
RRP	recommended retail price
SDK	Sub-Distributor Kecamatan
SME	small/medium-sized enterprise
SPSI	Serikat Pekerja Selurun Indonesia (All Indonesia Labour Union)
UI	Unilever Indonesia

Foreword: Oxfam

Oxfam[1] believes that the private sector can be an important engine of development. Companies, when they act responsibly, can play a vital role in contributing to sustainable development and poverty reduction.

Our reason for undertaking this particular research project with Unilever stems from our desire to deepen understanding, on the part of both Oxfam and Unilever, of the impacts of investment by a multinational company upon people living in poverty. For many years, foreign direct investment has been seen as being key to 'pro-poor' development for what it brings in terms of wealth creation, employment, technology transfer, and other components of poverty alleviation. Yet there is a wide on-going debate about whether and how these contributions translate into real benefits for people living in poverty.

Research on corporate environmental and social impacts often focuses upon a specific aspect of operations. Our aim with this project was to examine a company's impacts more comprehensively, and especially to investigate the furthest ends where poor people's interaction with the business are indirect, informal, and possibly most vulnerable to exploitation. By researching the spectrum of Unilever Indonesia's activities, we wanted to begin to describe the 'poverty footprint' of these activities. There is much more to do to develop a methodology that consistently makes poor people a visible and integral part of the analysis of the net impacts of a company's operations.

This project was a pilot, conducted in a very complex local setting. Through it we have gained a better understanding of the importance of considering the whole value chain, including the potential for distribution chains to generate employment and income. In the future a stronger rights-based approach, more gender-differentiated data, and a more 'people-centred' methodology would enhance our findings greatly. While the research did examine UI's interaction with Indonesians as consumers, workers, producers, and citizens, this was done in the main by 'looking out' from the company, rather than 'looking in' from the perspective of people living in poverty. Oxfam is pleased that this research has generated so much learning for ourselves and others on which to build in future work with the private sector.

This initiative prompted both Oxfam and Unilever to challenge their own biases and assumptions. We have assumed that engaging the private sector in a collaborative project can bring about positive change. Through intensive dialogue, Oxfam believes that it has succeeded in raising awareness with Unilever about the potential impacts of their business choices and operations, and that this may help Unilever and others to take into account 'pro-poor' opportunities in the future. Oxfam will continue its critical engagement with companies, as part of a broad range of influencing activities. This includes respecting the choice of others who have decided to stay out of such engagements.

This project has depended on the efforts of very different actors to work together to deepen understanding and identify some potential for real change. We hope that the insights provided will generate enthusiasm for trying to fill the gaps and improve on the methodology that we have begun to develop.

I thank all of our project team colleagues for their energy and commitment to the project. I am particularly grateful to Oxfam's team in Indonesia, and to the Unilever Indonesia team, for their hard work and willingness to welcome this international learning initiative.

Barbara Stocking

Director, Oxfam GB

Foreword: Unilever

The first question asked about this report is: why did you do it? The answer for Unilever is two-fold. First, our business engages in many ways with poor people around the world as producers and consumers. Second, the Millennium and Johannesburg Declarations (2000, 2002) place poverty eradication at the centre of global strategies for sustainable development. To play our part, and support the Declarations, we needed to increase understanding of the impact of the operations of a business like ours on the lives of poor people. Different industries interact in different ways with society. We believed that there were useful lessons to be learned from exploring how industry structure, operating practice, and, indeed, individual company values could, through wealth creation and the provision of goods and services, play a part in sustainable poverty reduction.

Our project partners, Oxfam GB in the UK and in Indonesia, Novib Oxfam Netherlands, and Jason Clay, the report author, brought a new perspective to our operations as we explored our interactions with Indonesian society. They have relentlessly challenged the impacts of the business model, the basis of management data, and the values behind our working practices. We have responded to these challenges step by step, creating in the process a growing body of shared information about our interactions with society, which this report describes. Not unexpectedly, it has not always been possible to reach agreement; where this is the case, the different viewpoints are stated. Nor did we believe that we needed to articulate a defence of all aspects of our business activity. This report offers a joint study of the complex reality of some key aspects of local business operations in a developing country, and the many opportunities that these present to support the development process.

At times it has been hard for our managers to find their values and behaviours subjected to such sceptical scrutiny, and to see their achievements, when operating in a complex business context, so lightly passed over. But as we have worked through the scepticism, there has been a growing realisation of two things: the passionate commitment on both sides; and the fact that, while the organisations have different starting points, both have a contribution to make.

This report is offered, not as an answer, but as a data-rich study of just one (albeit extraordinary) company, Unilever Indonesia, and its interactions with the people, business, and economy of just one (albeit extraordinary) country, Indonesia. It is the product of a learning partnership which demonstrated how much insight can be gained by working together. I hope that the desire to learn in a spirit of goodwill and common endeavour will be extended by the reader to this text, and that it will contribute to a greater understanding of the links between wealth creation and poverty reduction.

I am indebted to my predecessor, Niall FitzGerald, and Oxfam GB Director Barbara Stocking, who together inspired this joint research work, and to Maurits Lalisang and the team in Indonesia, in particular Tonny Pranatadjaja and Unilever Indonesia's former chairman, Nihal Kaviratne, for their unstinting support. I thank the project team in Indonesia, Europe, and the USA, who have worked so tirelessly for the project's success.

Patrick Cescau

Group Chief Executive, Unilever

Executive summary

Introduction

The business activities of multinational companies (MNCs) have an important contribution to make to economic development in developing countries. This contribution is particularly significant because the volume of private capital flows exceeds that of development assistance. International business activities and investments in developing countries have the potential to create positive or negative impacts at several levels for people living in poverty. The extent to which the wealth created by business can reduce poverty is determined by many factors. An industry's operating structure – and the values and strategies of individual companies within it – are critical factors. Likewise, the opportunities open to people living in poverty, and their negotiating power – as citizens, workers, producers, consumers, and community members – are key determinants in the local context.

It was in this context that a collaboration began between a major MNC, Unilever, and a large development and humanitarian organisation, Oxfam – two organisations with very different aims and perspectives. This research project attempted to create a space in which to increase understanding of the impacts of business on the lives of poor people, to inform the poverty-reduction debate. The project was intended to improve understanding among the wider business community, government, civil-society organisations, and academics about the relationship between a multinational business and poverty. As such, it was first and foremost a 'learning' project. The research does not purport to be comprehensive, and its scope is the operations of Unilever Indonesia (UI), not those of Unilever the multinational company.

This research explores to what extent, and how, the wealth generated by the local operating company of a multinational company in a developing country is translated into poverty impacts in one particular country, in this case Indonesia. The research focuses on Unilever Indonesia, the local operating company of Unilever, one of the world's leading fast-moving consumer-goods (FMCG) companies. UI has been active in Indonesia since 1933 (see Box A), and the majority of its goods are produced for the Indonesian market.

Despite its abundant natural and human resources, Indonesia has high levels of poverty, with more than 50 per cent of its population living on less than US$ 2 a day. Poor Indonesians face insecure livelihoods, a lack of access to basic services, limited opportunities for economic advancement, and a lack of power to influence their situation.

To explore the range of potential impacts, the research design was ambitious in scope, covering aspects of UI's entire value chain. Thus the report includes sections on the impacts of UI at the macro-economic level; UI's employment policies and practices; UI's relationships in its value chain from supply through distribution; UI's relationships with poor consumers in the marketplace; and UI's wider impact in the community, on the business sector and government in Indonesia.

Independent research undertaken in mid-2004 was supplemented with data from published documents produced by UI and Unilever, internal management documents used in day-to-day decision making, and information gathered from other sources. The in-depth partnership and joint research reflected here is a valuable addition to the more common corporate social responsibility (CSR) practice of public reporting.

Impacts at the macro-economic level

It is at the macro-economic level that the policies providing the basis for national poverty-reduction strategies are made: employment generation, strong public-sector investment, improved productivity, and macro-economic stability are among the foundations needed for economic development. Given the importance of these foundations, it is important to understand the impacts of foreign direct investment within this context. The macro-economic section of the research considered UI's contributions in terms of distribution of profits, shareholder dividends, taxes, balance of payments, overall employment figures, and behaviour during the financial crisis that began in 1997.

UI, as a part of an MNC but embedded in the local economy of a developing country, has significant forward and backward linkages into the local economy: for example, forward linkages through distribution networks and retailers, and backward linkages to suppliers. The majority of revenues generated by UI remain in Indonesia, through its local sourcing, wages, margins, and dividends to local shareholders (15 per cent of total dividends). Following an earlier period of investment by the parent company, inward investment flows from outside Indonesia were nil in recent years: a result of the profitability of the local business.

Box A: A brief history of Unilever in Indonesia

UI was founded in 1933. By 2003 the company had sales of US$ 984 million, around 84 per cent of which were home and personal care items such as soap powder, household cleaning products, hand soap, and shampoos. Around 16 per cent of sales were accounted for by foods such as tea, margarine, and ice cream. Unilever estimates that at least 95 per cent of Indonesians use one or more UI products each year, and that 90 per cent of poor people in Indonesia buy UI products in the course of a year. UI is ranked as the thirteenth-largest company by sales in Indonesia and the fourth-largest company in the FMCG sector.

For the five-year period beginning in 1999, 25 per cent (US$ 182 million) of UI's total pre-tax profits were retained and reinvested in local business activities. These funds represent an investment in UI's long-term future, as well as an investment in Indonesia's long-term development, particularly in the manufacturing and distribution sectors.

Of the remaining 1999–2003 pre-tax profits, 30 per cent (US$ 215m) went to government as corporation tax, and 45 per cent of profits were paid out as dividends to shareholders, the majority of whom are overseas investors. Excluding exports of tea and palm oil purchased from Indonesia by Unilever centrally, UI contributed to Indonesia's balance-of-payments deficit in this period. Because UI imports inputs and purchases foreign currency for its business operations, and remits dividends to shareholders outside the country (85 per cent), there is a net outflow of funds, showing that even a locally based company like UI with only modest exports can have a negative foreign-exchange impact on the country.

Total taxes paid to the Indonesian government were considerable, averaging about US$ 130 million per year, or about 19 per cent of company revenues over the five-year period. While the ultimate impacts of tax revenues on development and poverty in Indonesia depend on the policy choices of the Indonesian government, it is clear that a company such as UI can represent a substantial source of public revenue, and an early contributor to the development of the formal economy.

UI maintained its operations in Indonesia through the financial crisis of 1997–98, and its behaviour during this time offers an interesting case study. For example, UI adapted its business model to ensure that products remained affordable; renegotiated contracts with suppliers to maintain business for all parties; prioritised the retention of employees; and expanded local operations through joint ventures and acquisitions.

While it is difficult to use macro-economic indicators to measure the direct impact of UI's activities on people living below the poverty line, indirect positive impacts can be assumed in the contributions to government revenue; the stability of UI's value chain in a turbulent economy, with its attendant employment benefits; and an overall business model that is deeply embedded in the Indonesian economy. The potentially negative impact of the outflow of UI funds on people living in poverty in Indonesia was not possible to measure. A deeper understanding of poverty impacts, therefore, requires a more direct analysis of UI's operations and its relationships with employees, suppliers, distributors, retailers, and consumers.

Employment impacts

Many developing countries, including Indonesia, face significant rates of underemployment and unemployment. MNCs can have an impact on employment because of their size and their reach into the local economy. Assessing the impact of employment on poverty is more than a matter of numerical quantification. Although that is an important first step, the assessment also involves ascertaining whether people, through their employment, gain skills and confidence that empower them to build economic security, accumulate assets, and make sustainable improvements in their lives. Much of the debate about corporate social responsibility has focused on the role of MNCs as direct employers. This section of the research considers UI's principles and values, and the extent to which the company takes responsibility for maintaining its standards among its own employees and contract workers.

UI's business structure consists of a core workforce of about 5,000 people, of whom about 60 per cent are employees, most of them permanent, and just under 40 per cent are contract workers, employed directly or through contracting agencies. Beyond this is a well-established network of suppliers, distributors, and retailers which is described in Chapter 4 of this report.

UI sets high standards for the treatment of its permanent employees. It adheres to the Unilever (global) Code of Business Principles. Pay and benefits are above what is required by law, positioning UI in the top quartile of Indonesian companies. In terms of policy and practice, there are high health and safety standards, good retirement and maternity benefits and workplace facilities, and a strong emphasis on training. All UI employees have a written contract, and there are clear procedures for negotiations between workers and management.

The closer and more formally workers are linked with UI's operations, the more they benefit directly from the company. In the period studied (2003/2004), the number of contract workers engaged by UI grew as a proportion of employees, because more workers were needed to cover periods of change at two UI sites. While future trends in contract employment at UI are unclear, Oxfam is concerned that the number of contract workers functioning within UI is significant, at around 40 per cent of the workforce in 2003. Although contract employment is recognised as an integral part of UI's business strategy, the research indicated two respects in which the application of standards needs improvement, on which UI is committed to take action. One of these is the need to ensure that UI's labour-supply companies observe legal requirements concerning the transfer of temporary employees to permanent employment contracts; the other is the need to respond to the concerns raised by a female contract worker that illness or pregnancy could result in loss of employment. These cases illustrated how contracting out employment may reduce a company's ability to monitor the situation of contract workers or suppliers' employees, and thus result in gaps between corporate policy and practice in respect of these workers.

The value chain from supply through distribution

The business operations of a large company like UI are at the centre of a long and complex value chain with both forward and backward linkages. This section of the research aimed to assess the extent to which the producers and suppliers (backward linkages) and distributors and retailers (forward linkages) who are linked to UI through its value chain are able to participate in the benefits of UI's success. The creation of value, income, assets, and employment in itself is not necessarily an indicator of positive impacts for people living in poverty: this depends on how the benefits of the value chain are distributed, which depends in turn on other factors, an important one being their bargaining power within dynamic markets for raw materials and labour.

Supplier companies

UI purchases the majority of goods and services for its business operations through a local supply chain consisting of a large network of more than 300 supplier companies. UI's business model over the past two decades has come to focus on high-volume, high-technology, and high-value-added operations, while other parts of the business became independent operations or were outsourced. In this way, UI was able to expand its business while at the same time building production capacity among independent companies.

In 2003, UI purchased goods and services valued at more than US$ 254 million, mostly from Indonesian companies. Many of these supplier companies were originally set up by UI, and (while direct ties are reduced over time) relationships between them tend to last for many years. Almost all these companies have contracts for 6–12 months. UI has boosted the quality and standards of local manufacturing, through technical assistance programmes and the extension of UI's quality-management systems throughout the supply chain.

UI's investment in local suppliers ensures a steady supply of high-quality inputs for the company, while creating local jobs, assets, profits, and tax revenues. This represents both an ingredient of UI's success and a major economic-multiplier effect of UI's investment.

The major benefit for companies of being in UI's value chain is a predictable market with high volume sales, and UI's reliability in paying them. Yet negotiating prices with UI, and the need to comply with stringent quality requirements, may be challenging for local supplier companies.

The research showed that supplier companies exceed legal regulations governing wages and benefits in Indonesia, but the pay and employment conditions for suppliers' employees and contract workers were lower than the levels among UI's direct workforce. Like UI, supplier companies employ contract workers within their workforce, and this raises some of the same issues that relate to contract workers within UI.

Producers of raw materials

The home and personal-care and food products that UI sells are made from a wide range of industrial and agricultural raw materials, sourced from many different producers, traders, and processors. The small-scale agricultural producers who grow the crops such as coconut, sugar, and black soybeans are among the poorest people in UI's value chain, so changes in their situation can have considerable impacts on their livelihoods. The value generated by the goods that they produce must be shared among a large number of supply-chain actors, of whom they are usually the least powerful. The indirect relationship also makes it difficult for a purchasing company like UI to influence producer conditions.

This research included a case study of the production of a brand that UI had acquired recently: Kecap Bango, a sweet soy sauce made from black soybeans and coconut sugar. Because sales of Kecap Bango are growing rapidly, UI needed to find a steady and consistent supply of high-quality black soybeans. In partnership with researchers at a local university, the company started to work with a small group of producers, offering them three things that they valued: security of market for their product; credit; and technical assistance. In good harvest years the producers also get a better return on investment and labour than they do from other crops that they might grow. Both UI and the producers have benefited from this arrangement, and the number of farmers wanting to participate has grown steadily.

However, there are some problems with the black-soybean pilot scheme, the most important being the fact that the farmers bear a major financial risk within this new contracting arrangement, and the fact that UI's strength as a large company limits farmers' negotiating power. Moreover, the success of farmers selling this 'niche' product cannot be easily replicated if there is not a 'business case' for it. This holds true for crops for which there is greater supply than demand, such as the other ingredient of Kecap Bango: coconut sugar. Still, the case is very useful in increasing understanding of different perspectives and impacts within UI's value chain. Such an understanding, if combined with a search for more business cases that also increase the value-adding potential and hence power of poor producers, could enhance the longer-term trading partnerships between agricultural producers and large companies.

The alternative black-soybean supply chain established by UI removes layers of middlemen, thus creating potential for increasing producers' incomes. In this and other ways, companies or buyers can increase incomes or promote savings among producers. Opportunities to do this include direct purchasing at higher prices, pre-financing production, and direct bargaining on prices between producers (or producer associations) and buyers.

Distributors

UI's complex distribution chain consists of a mixture of wholesalers and 'modern' retailers (self-service stores and supermarkets) and 'traditional' or 'general' retailers and vendors. It extends to small shops, family-owned *warungs* (small sales outlets inside family houses), kiosks, and street hawkers. It is striking that more people are employed, and more value is generated, on the distribution side of the value chain than on the supply side. It is also notable that employment generation in distribution is often overlooked as having a potential contribution to make to economic development.

UI's expansion in marketing small sachets to low-income consumers benefited the company by increasing its overall sales and market penetration, and also increased employment through the distribution system. It is estimated that up to 1.8 million small stores and street vendors sell UI products informally in rural markets and poor urban areas. So even when a product does not have a particularly large impact on employment or income on the supply side, it can still have an impact through distribution. UI's sales also contributed generally to the development of an independent distribution and retail sector in Indonesia.

As with the supply chain, the research indicated that the closer to UI the distributors and modern retailers are in the chain, the more likely they are to be able to negotiate better prices, gain skills and knowledge, enjoy higher pay and better employment conditions, and thus sustainably improve their lives. At the very edge of the formal economy, where poor families run small retail activities that may represent up to 40 per cent of the family income, both incomes and standards of product handling and storage tend to be lower. To an even greater extent than the supply chain, the local multiplier impact of the distribution chain is little understood.

The overall value chain

Overall, the research estimates that the full-time equivalent (FTE) of about 300,000 people make their livelihoods from UI's value chain. Strikingly, more than half of this employment is found in UI's distribution and retail chain, with about one third in the supply chain.

Job creation is only one way to assess the economic impacts of the value chain. Another is to seek a monetary indicator, in this case gross margins along the value chain, as a proxy for the financial value created by each group of participants in the chain. The total value generated along the UI value chain is conservatively estimated at US$ 633 million. Of this, UI earns about US$ 212 million on the value that it creates as a key player in the value chain; the remaining US$ 421 million is distributed among other actors in the chain. The value added within the value chain is even more dispersed than the benefits of employment within the chain.

Direct UI operations account for about 34 per cent of the total value generated throughout the supply chain, while taxes paid to government by UI represent 26 per cent, retail operations about 18 per cent, suppliers about 9 per cent, distributors 6 per cent, farmers about 4 per cent, and advertising and other expenses 3 per cent. The total value captured declines towards either end of the value chain. The value captured by poorer people working at either end of the value chain, especially primary producers at the supply end, is much lower than the value captured by those who are in direct interaction with UI and closer to the centre of UI's value chain. The value captured by those people working at the ends of the value chain increases where they have a stronger negotiating position in relation to their product or service, where value chains are restructured to change the distribution of benefits, or where they can increase the value of their products or services, for example through innovation.

Low-income consumers in the marketplace

International FMCG companies are increasingly reaching out to people living on low incomes around the world. The result is an increase in the worldwide consumer base for MNCs, and an increased use of branded products by people on low incomes. This part of the research reviewed four areas:

- access to UI products, including the types of purchaser, pricing, and market share
- the role of brands in the marketplace
- the role of promotion and advertising
- the extent to which companies like UI are meeting, or creating, needs for poor consumers.

This was a particularly challenging aspect of the overall project, given Oxfam's and Unilever's very different approaches and attitudes to these issues at the outset, and the fast-changing market dynamics that affect a company like UI. The findings are important nevertheless, as lessons for Oxfam and Unilever, and as points of departure for further work in this area by other companies and organisations.

According to UI data, 95 per cent of Indonesians use at least one UI product, across all socio-economic groups. Many of UI's product sales represent basic goods, such as hand soap, laundry products, and tea. People on low incomes tend to spend a larger portion of their income on FMCGs than those with higher incomes. Many of UI's products have become more affordable for people living in poverty in recent years, in part because they are sold in smaller packages, called 'sachets'. While the unit cost is higher, owing to packaging and distribution costs that are reflected in the sale price, this marketing strategy responds to the reality that people on low incomes have limited cash in hand.

The FMCG industry in Indonesia is highly competitive, and within it UI leads in market share in some categories, like toothpaste and hair care, while in other categories, such as powder detergents, local companies lead. UI's recent success is in part based on the expansion of sachet packaging, and the very extensive distribution network for UI products that reaches into all parts of a very large country. UI aims to provide low-income consumers with access to products that are of consistently high quality and value. Moreover, UI's partnerships with a range of producer companies and distributors mean that its expansion supports employment within the local economy.

UI's success and expansion as a company raises questions for Oxfam about whether UI is displacing smaller-scale local producers, ultimately constraining competition in the marketplace, rather than stimulating it. Oxfam endorses the view that a good industrial policy for developing countries includes nurturing the ability of independent small producers to compete successfully with global brands in the local marketplace. Such competition does exist in Indonesian FMCG markets: while UI market share has grown during the period under review, the number of companies in the market has also grown. However, within this project it was difficult to judge the overall balance of market share between international and locally owned businesses across the wide range of product categories provided by the industry. Equally important, Oxfam questions whether companies like UI may be creating rather than meeting needs for poor consumers, and over time turning luxuries into necessities through advertising and promotion.

It was impossible to measure the overall benefit or loss for either poor consumers or small-scale local producers resulting from UI's increasing market share and success within the FMCG industry. What is clear, however, is that other companies learn from UI's marketing strategies, and will have to keep up with it in order to compete successfully within the sector.

Determining impacts on poor consumers through their purchase of UI products, especially trying to compare them with alternative purchases, was equally difficult. Many consumers within each socio-economic group are influenced by the 'image' of a brand. If local non-branded items are becoming less common, how much is this due to marketing and distribution versus better value for money? Given the wide prevalence of both TV and print, responsible standards of advertising and good communication links with people at all socio-economic levels – both of them important aims of UI – are at least two benchmarks for social responsibility.

UI's wider impact in the community

UI's wider impact in the community was briefly considered, in terms of both corporate community involvement and UI's influence on government and the business community more widely. UI invests in a wide range of philanthropic activities, often linked to an aspect of its business expertise. Oxfam and Unilever agree that the greatest potential for pro-poor impacts lies within UI's mainstream operations and value chain. Nonetheless, voluntary community involvement can also provide a positive interaction with society, bringing benefits to communities and directly and indirectly to the business itself.

UI's main influence on other businesses has been among its own business partners, which often support similar activities, and which appear to have adopted UI's practices in other respects, such as health and safety standards. One identifiable area of UI's influence in society was in taking a public stand against corruption, for which UI has been cited by other NGOs.

Conclusions

In concluding the report, Oxfam and Unilever set out what each organisation has learned from the research and from the process of working together. A selection of key lessons learned by each organisation is presented in Boxes B and C. Feedback from our external reference group helped to shape the final report, and some of the group's questions and suggestions are highlighted in Chapter 7. The report concludes with an indication of further topics for research, and some next steps for both Oxfam and Unilever.

In the end, both organisations came to realise that, despite their very different missions and goals, they share a common commitment to contributing to poverty reduction and development. By the end of the project both Oxfam and Unilever were much closer to understanding the limitations and opportunities that determine what companies can and cannot be expected to do to contribute to poverty reduction.

Box B: A selection of Oxfam's lessons from the research

- We learned that our analysis needs to be more alert to the differences between multinational companies. At every point in its value chain, UI's business is highly dependent on Indonesians: as producers, suppliers, employees, contract workers, distributors, retailers, and consumers. UI's business decisions and choices reflect the embedded nature of its operations, favouring a long-term approach to optimising opportunities for business success, and an emphasis on the development of skills and industry within the wider Indonesian economy. As such, UI is very different from some of the traditional targets of CSO campaigning, such as extractive or export-processing industries. These differences have important implications for an understanding of UI's poverty footprint; moreover, an appreciation of them can help us to understand why and how a company like UI might be motivated to study and improve its poverty impacts. Our findings suggest that highly embedded MNCs and large domestic companies might in future provide a focus for useful work on private-sector poverty impacts and poverty-reduction strategies. While there is an increasing number of corporate social responsibility measures in

place, there is nothing that allows companies to conduct a systematic assessment of their positive and negative contributions to poverty reduction throughout the value chain. This project has increased our understanding of UI's poverty footprint in Indonesia. It also provides the company with some insights into how they can increase their overall contribution to poverty reduction and perhaps eventually develop a 'pro-poor' policy. This is a powerful concept, which may be useful for engagement with other companies.

- We have gained a better understanding of the potential of distribution chains to generate employment and income. Our research found that for every direct employee there were many more jobs in distribution chains. For NGOs currently focusing their efforts on improving conditions for producers and other workers within supply chains, the research shows that it may also be valuable to analyse MNC policies towards the distribution and retail aspect of their value chains.

- However, as a result of this project, it became clearer that participation in value chains alone does not guarantee improvements in the living conditions of poor people.

This reinforced our belief that for value chains to work for poor people, there need to be other social institutions and resources in place, such as credit and saving schemes, marketing associations, and insurance schemes, as well as diversification of income streams, to avoid dependency on any single company or market.

- We also learned how difficult it is to reach a specific definition of what constitutes 'fair practice' by companies. This issue is not as clearly defined as we would like it to be. For example, despite international definitions of 'a living wage' and how to calculate it, and despite the national definition of a legal minimum wage, it remains difficult to judge the appropriateness of MNC wage levels within a given context. For example, how much above the legally required minimum wage is it appropriate for an MNC to pay? And to what extent can the same policies be encouraged for an MNC's suppliers and contractors? Similarly we debated, but did not resolve, the concept of a 'fair price' and the question of how much expenditure on advertising is appropriate as a proportion of consumer prices.

Box C: A selection of Unilever's lessons from the research

- The primary lesson for us is the insight that we gained into the extent of the widespread 'job' multiplier in UI's total value chain. While admittedly the FTE calculations in this report are estimates, the findings nonetheless point to the potential use of value-chain policies as a tool in sustainable poverty reduction. As such it will be useful to share the insights of the FMCG value-chain multiplier, and the opportunities that it offers, with all those concerned with poverty-reduction strategies.

- The spread of value-adding activity throughout the value chain creates a broad tax base. A predictable tax base is essential for the development of the formal economy on which the government can build, and finance, its social and environmental programmes. This report addresses only the direct taxes paid by UI to the Indonesian government. Further research could explore the scale of taxes paid by the many players involved in an FMCG value chain, including both companies and individual workers.

- FMCG value chains can offer poor people an opportunity to gain basic skills within a structured learning environment and earn incremental, regular income. Although imperfect, these opportunities in turn may be the first steps towards accumulating assets, increasing independence, and improving quality of life. Oxfam has pointed out that there may be negative impacts for poor people who participate in FMCG value chains, such as poor working terms and conditions, or debt and financing difficulties. These are matters that need particular care and attention. Government, businesses, and civil-society organisations can each play a part in helping to gain the best outcomes for poor people.

- Even where there is a shared appreciation of the benefits of an alternative supply chain, as in the black-soybean project, it is recognised that there are constraints and limitations on the viability of the model, and doubts about whether the model itself represents the answer to the problems of poor farmers. Where it can, Unilever will continue to work with a wide range of partners, including NGOs, to seek better, sustainable practices to reduce negative social and environmental impacts in the production of the agricultural crops that it purchases.

- A persistent focus on the position of the individual living in poverty – whether man, woman, or child – is essential for developing sustainable poverty-reduction strategies. Oxfam held the line on this matter throughout the project, and the Unilever team acknowledged its importance. For a company like UI which interacts with people living in poverty, this mindset and the feedback that it creates offer an opportunity to increase the positive impacts of its activities and reduce the negative impacts. It also indicates that while a company has an important 'product-delivering, wealth-creating, skills-transferring' role, it is only one participant along-side other businesses, governments, international institutions, and civil-society organisations in the drive for sustainable poverty reduction. For optimum impact, a concerted effort is required.

1 Introduction

Why Oxfam and Unilever began this project

Combining their insight and expertise in business, participatory development, and public policy, Unilever and Oxfam[1] are working together to explore the links between wealth creation and poverty reduction, aiming to make a contribution to sustainable poverty reduction.[2]

Around the world, significantly more money is transferred between countries through global private-sector capital flows than through development assistance. From 2000 to 2003, global net private capital flows averaged more than US$ 200 billion per year (UNCTAD 2003). Public flows of official development assistance, by comparison, totalled only US$ 58 billion per year. It is important to consider how private capital flows, and foreign direct investment in particular, can make a positive contribution to reducing poverty. The ILO-convened World Commission on the Social Dimension of Globalization has found that people around the world view globalisation (and, by extension, some of the activities of international companies) as positive or negative insofar as it has a positive or negative impact on their own livelihoods.

For development and poverty reduction, wealth creation through the production and provision of goods and services is vital; and business, because it can create wealth, has a key role to play. But when business activity adds to the wealth of a developing country, it does not necessarily result in the reduction of poverty for the many. Wealth creation needs to be accompanied by public policies and incentives that enable people living in poverty or on very low incomes to participate successfully in markets.

Neither Unilever nor Oxfam has undertaken a research project like this before. When setting it up, both viewed it as an opportunity to learn from each other, as well as to create shared insights which both organisations could disseminate and use more broadly themselves.

Unilever believes that the project will help it to understand its business impacts on people living in poverty in Indonesia, and to explore how the wealth, employment, and products that the company creates could better benefit that part of society. As the value chains of international businesses extend more deeply within national and local economies, such businesses have an increasing degree of contact, both direct and indirect, with poor people, particularly in low-income countries. Many companies seeking to operate in markets where poverty is widespread need a better understanding of poverty-related issues, and want to understand how enterprises can reduce or compound the problems that poor people face.

Civil-society organisations (CSOs)[3] like Oxfam, working to influence the private sector, need to understand how international business works, in order to identify opportunities for overcoming poverty and promoting sustainable development. Oxfam expects an important outcome of the work to be a sharpening of its ability to understand the nuances of pro-poor strategies in the private sector and to engage more effectively with companies in general.

Many CSOs are sceptical about the potential for multinational companies (MNCs) to have positive impacts on poverty. They note that companies can reach people living in poverty as consumers (at the so-called 'bottom of the pyramid') and as producers of primary agricultural products; but they expect companies' pursuit of profits to be damaging to poor communities. Likewise, some argue that MNCs marginalise local entrepreneurs and small-scale competitors, thereby undermining local economies and traditional employment. They argue that MNCs rarely support local entrepreneurs to generate income and jobs. For the more critical CSOs, selling branded products to the poor is little more than an attempt by MNCs to capture the income of the poor without giving anything in return.

At the other end of the spectrum, many investors and corporate executives believe that foreign direct investment will automatically benefit the host country. They argue that all jobs related to the company's activities are additional jobs created, and that technology, skills, and expertise will be transferred to local workers and companies. They believe that investment by multinational companies will help the country to be better integrated into the global economy and so, directly or indirectly, will help to reduce poverty. They argue, therefore, that host countries should welcome such investment, no matter how much or how little of the wealth that it generates is retained within the country.

There are examples around the world of poor countries and communities that have suffered many of the negative impacts described above, while others have benefited significantly from the positive impacts. Oxfam and Unilever recognise that this is because all foreign direct investment is not alike.

Box 1: Unilever and Oxfam

Unilever is a business whose worldwide mission is to 'add vitality to life', 'to meet everyday needs for nutrition, hygiene, and personal care, with brands that help people feel good, look good, and get more out of life'. The company has operations in around 100 countries, and its brands are on sale in around 50 more. As a business committed to long-term sustainable growth, Unilever regards profitability as a key measure of success and an essential ingredient of sustainability. Unilever has extensive experience of working in developing economies with low-income consumers.

Oxfam is an independent, non-profit, non-government organisation (NGO) whose mission is to work with others to overcome poverty and suffering worldwide. Oxfam's experience at the community level is matched by its campaigning and advocacy work to change the policies that prevent people from escaping poverty. Oxfam's work in more than 70 developing countries brings it into day-to-day contact with some of the poorest people in the world, and gives it a deep understanding of the challenges that they face. Through its support for local communities and its advocacy work,

Oxfam helps to create the conditions in which poor people have better opportunities for sustainable development. Oxfam's engagement with the private sector is driven by the knowledge that business plays a crucial role in driving development. Through its advocacy, campaigning, and programme work, Oxfam seeks to influence companies to adopt policies and practices that ensure that their core business activities contribute to and do not undermine poor people's ability to lift themselves out of poverty.

What is this research about?

This research explores to what extent, and how, the activities and wealth generated by the local operating company of an MNC in a developing country are translated into reduced poverty: for example, through employment or asset creation, increased skills and raised standards, local sustainable purchasing policies, or the provision of consumer goods. This report provides an overview of the links between the Unilever Indonesia (UI) business model and poverty reduction. It is based on research which focused on the following four areas:

- mapping the impacts of UI at the 'macro-economic' level
- exploring UI's policies and practices
- analysing supply-chain relationships and issues
- understanding the implications of UI in the marketplace.

Box 2: The challenge of definitions

During the course of this project, it became clear that defining the terms 'multinational company' (MNC) and 'foreign direct investment' (FDI) was not straightforward.

In this report, the global company Unilever is described as an MNC. However, this report focuses on the operations of Unilever Indonesia (UI), which has existed for more than 70 years as a local operating company within the global Unilever family. For this reason,

Unilever describes itself as a 'multi-local multinational'.

In the past, Unilever has invested a large amount of money in building up its business (UI) in Indonesia. However, since 1981, when UI went public and 15 per cent of the shares were acquired locally and 85 per cent were retained by the parent company in the Netherlands, capital for the growth of the business has come from local earnings and retained profits, rather than from the Netherlands.

This profitable local business has not needed to call upon new capital infusions from Europe.

Nevertheless, UI's operations should still be considered as a form of foreign direct investment, albeit in an advanced state where dividends flow out of the country but investment capital does not necessarily flow in.

The project was not intended to evaluate UI in order to audit or judge its operations, but rather to improve understanding among the wider business community, government, civil-society organisations, and academics about the relationship between a multinational business and poverty, by analysing one example of how business and poverty interrelate. As such, it was first and foremost a 'learning' project. Moreover, it is important to recognise the extent to which businesses operating in any context are enabled and constrained by government policy. A full investigation of this and other external conditions affecting UI's business operations in Indonesia was beyond the scope of the research. This case raises as many questions as it answers, but nevertheless it should help those interested in these issues to understand the complexities of the subject and to formulate more precise questions for further research.

Methodology

In 2003, Unilever and Oxfam signed a Statement of Intent and Memorandum of Understanding (MOU) which defined the project's scope and purpose.[4] Through this process they discussed research topics, as well as possible locations for research. The focus was narrowed to East Asia, then to Indonesia – a country rich in human and natural resources, but facing huge challenges in providing opportunities and stability in terms of employment and social services. Oxfam has a long-established programme in Indonesia, and Unilever has long-standing operations there through the UI business.

The two parties agreed to examine activities along UI's entire value chain,[5] from sourcing of raw materials to the impacts on consumers who purchase UI's products. This had the advantage of giving an overview of this fast-moving consumer-goods (FMCG) company within Indonesia. Within the value-chain analysis, one labour-intensive agricultural product (the sweet soy sauce, Kecap Bango, pronounced 'ketchap bango'), was selected as a case study. Some of the major products sourced by Unilever in Indonesia, including tea and palm oil, were not studied in depth in this report, primarily because Unilever is exploring them through other initiatives.[6] The value of these exports is not included in the resource-flow figures given in the section on the macro-economic impacts of UI in Chapter 2.

Staff from Unilever and Oxfam formed a project team, which was supported by The Corporate Citizenship Company (retained by Unilever), an independent report author, Jason Clay, and four independent Indonesian research teams (see Appendix 1 for a complete list). The research teams and the report author were jointly selected and funded by Oxfam and Unilever. Both organisations nominated individuals for an external reference group, eventually comprising 11 members (see Appendix 1). Terms of reference for a study of four components of the UI business were drafted, discussed, revised, and agreed.

The four research components, as originally specified, were as follows:

- **Impacts of UI at the macro-economic level:** this component was intended as a context-setting piece. It assesses how the local operations of an MNC like Unilever could be beneficial to the economy generally, and thereby broadly support human development in Indonesia (for example, through providing employment and generating tax revenue), and to what extent poor people share in these benefits.

- **Exploration of UI's policies and practices:** this research explored (a) whether UI's policies and practices are effective in maintaining and raising the standards of UI, its suppliers, and its customer companies, and (b) whether these standards have positive benefits for society in general and poor people in particular.

- **Analysis of the supply chain:** this component considered whether poor people in Indonesia could benefit from participation in the supply chains of UI. It included a study of one product in particular: the sweet soy sauce, Kecap Bango.

- **UI's impacts on the poor in the marketplace:** this component considered whether UI provides consumers with greater informed choice and increased access to important everyday consumer goods, resulting in reduced vulnerability and improved quality of life. It also assessed the impact of a dispersed, locally rooted marketing and distribution network.

Between February and June 2004, independent primary research was undertaken within these four research areas. Data were collected and organised by four teams working simultaneously. During the research it became clear that it would not be possible to address within the timeframe all the points set out above. The four resulting background papers, the themes that they addressed, and the data that they presented formed the basis for many of the insights and findings presented in this report.

The sources of data used in this report consist of the following:

- the independent background papers that were commissioned
- the public documents of UI and Unilever
- internal management documents of UI
- emails and other written and verbal communications, primarily from Unilever staff
- published data from other sources.

Internal information was sourced from management data systems used in the day-to-day operations of the business, shared in good faith as the information on which policy and management decisions in UI are made. Unless otherwise noted, all financial and personnel figures in this report come from UI internal management reports. The research findings are based on UI 2003 data, unless otherwise specified.

Several distinct components were central to the project:

- The process of drawing up and negotiating the terms of reference, and commissioning and reviewing the four background papers, was itself a source of learning for both Unilever and Oxfam. Discussion of the background research was the beginning of an intensive process of fact-finding and discussion.

- Globally, Unilever has established a process of 'self-assessment' and 'positive assurance' to manage and report on corporate responsibility around the world. CSOs are generally wary of corporate self-assessment, because they think that companies are less able than independent auditors to extract sensitive information objectively and credibly. Oxfam's experience is that a multi-stakeholder dialogue with credible local experts, such as trade unions and labour-rights NGOs, is most effective for assessment. However, Unilever and Oxfam agree that internal control processes such as positive assurance are an essential basis for sound data collection and external reporting, and may be combined effectively with external reviews. Unilever has found that self-assessment and positive assurance is an effective tool for engaging managers in improving overall performance on environmental and social issues.

- This research project was the first time that Unilever had invited an NGO to review its internal documents and interview a range of local employees. Despite problems of small sample size and imperfect data sets, the findings in this report are illuminating and reasonably robust, demonstrating new ways to assess the impacts of an MNC on poverty reduction. Where it was impossible to verify information well enough to satisfy the external author or Oxfam, or where there were clearly different perspectives on the interpretation of a piece of information, this has been reflected openly in the report.

The research does not purport to be comprehensive or, in many cases, representative of UI's operations for different product lines. The scope of this research is the operations of UI, not those of Unilever the multinational company.

This research represents a data-rich, and therefore substantial, contribution to the often polarised debate about whether MNCs, and globalisation more generally, benefit poor people. The process itself provided insights into how to identify principles of engagement between different stakeholders wishing to develop pro-poor strategies. This research and analysis address complex and often sensitive issues. Open-mindedness, transparency, and honesty have been essential, both in defining and undertaking the work and in analysing and reporting the results here.

Both Unilever and Oxfam were aware of the risks inherent in undertaking this joint project, given the ambitious nature of the research and the volume of criticism concerning multinational corporate activity in Indonesia and around the world. Unilever shared confidential company information with all members of the project team, subject to agreements reached on confidentiality rules. A series of meetings, teleconferences, and visits included a frank exchange of information and opinions, based as far as possible on evidence presented in research and company data. This in turn fostered a genuine partnership and trust within the project team, especially when discussing dilemmas and trade-offs. Both organisations agree that this type of in-depth partnership and joint research is a valuable addition to the more common corporate social responsibility (CSR) practice of public reporting.

Data for this report were gathered from more than 400 individuals, through interviews with a broad range of stakeholders, including UI management; UI joint-venture partners; representatives of companies with whom UI has direct contacts (such as suppliers, distributors, sub-distributors, advertising agencies); and individuals who are part of UI's value chain but do not have direct contact with the company (such as raw-material producers, suppliers, retailers, and workers who are employed for raw-material production or at the retail level). Additional information and opinions were gathered in focus groups and from individuals and organisations unrelated to UI. Finally, data for the report were also gleaned from an extensive review of dozens of published sources and internal company reports.

During the writing of the report, a number of gaps in the data became apparent. The authors and reviewers of the drafts asked researchers to clarify points or even gather new data. Nine drafts were prepared, often with several versions of each before a draft was completed and submitted for comment. The drafting process was difficult, because the report had to address the facts of the case, as well as their interpretation by both Oxfam and Unilever. Often there were multiple interpretations of the same data within each organisation. Five meetings were held to discuss various drafts and gaps in the data, or areas of disagreement about either the facts or their interpretation. The seventh draft was sent to external stakeholders for review. Their feedback was incorporated into the eighth draft. A final meeting was held in Oxford in May 2005 to provide feedback for the ninth and final draft.

While this research was admittedly limited in many ways, it was rigorous. To date there are limited case studies analysing the impacts and reverberations of a multinational company's operations and strategies throughout the value chain in a developing country, from raw-material producers to consumers. This report represents a joint effort by Oxfam and Unilever to provide information where previously little or none existed. Undoubtedly, much more work is needed on these issues. It is our hope that this research and report will be used as a guide to extend understanding of these issues.

The context of the research project

Poverty in Indonesia

In 2002, the population of Indonesia was about 213 million. Population growth from 1998 to 2002 was 1.2 per cent (Economist Intelligence Unit 2003). Despite abundant natural resources and great wealth among some of its population, in 2002 more than 25 per cent of children under the age of five were malnourished, and some 15 per cent of the population did not live to the age of 40 (National Human Development Report 2004). Nearly 45 per cent of the population do not have access to clean water, and 23 per cent do not have access to health facilities. Some 79.3 per cent of children stay in school until they are 13–15 years of age, and 49.9 per cent until they are 16–18 years of age.

International definitions of poverty are generally equivalent to US$ 1 or US$ 2 per person per day. Many countries develop their own national definitions as well. Table 1 shows the proportions of people living in poverty in Indonesia in 1996, 1999, and 2002, according to three definitions of poverty. Poverty levels in Indonesia rose after the 1997–98 economic crisis and have fallen again in the last few years. This report, when discussing poor people and poverty, refers to the people – approximately 50 per cent of the population of Indonesia – who live on US$ 2 or less per day.[7]

Table 1: Percentage of people living in poverty in Indonesia (1996, 1999, 2002)

	1996	1999	2002
According to international poverty line of US$ 2 or less/day	50.5%	65.1%	53.4%
According to international poverty line of US$ 1 or less/day	7.8%	12.0%	7.4%
According to Indonesian government data, using a National Poverty Line (monetised at about US$ 1.50/day)	17.5%	23.4%	18.2%

Source: World Bank Indonesia, December 2003

Box 3: Oxfam's view of poverty

Oxfam believes that poverty is not simply a function of income levels. It also depends on people's real and perceived access to opportunity, as well as their ability to negotiate for themselves, to create and maintain assets, and to be secure in their livelihoods. Poverty both is, and stems from, a denial of the basic rights to which every human being is entitled — such as food, education, and civil and political freedoms. People living in poverty experience a combination of low income, few assets, insufficient skills, and limited opportunities or power to change their circumstances for the better. Poverty makes people more vulnerable to the effects of conflict and natural disasters, as well as to marginalisation by factors of race, ethnicity, religion, or gender. Business may have a direct or indirect impact on these basic rights, the most obvious being labour rights. This means that income levels and the $2 per person per day poverty line alone are very limited indicators of whether or not a household is (or perceives itself) to be poor. It also explains the growing interest (within the private sector and elsewhere) in other poverty indicators that are used to track progress towards the Millennium Development Goals.

Since 1996, the government of Indonesia has defined and calculated a 'minimum subsistence need' (Kebutuhan Hidup Minimum, KHM) – a bundle of 43 consumption items that are deemed essential to meet the livelihood needs of a single worker. These include food, clothing, housing, transport, health services, and recreation. The legal minimum wage[8] in Indonesia is calculated at only 90 per cent of the KHM, so that workers earning the minimum wage are still unlikely to accumulate assets or improve their lives or those of their families. The implications of this for companies aiming to ensure a living wage for those working in their value chains are discussed further in Chapters 3 and 4.

1998 was a defining year in Indonesia's recent history. The country's growth rate collapsed, from growth of 7 to 8 per cent per year in the early 1990s to a negative 13.8 per cent in 1998. Similarly, inflation, which had ranged between 5 and 10 per cent in the early 1990s, soared to 58 per cent in 1998 (IMF 2004). After decades of gradually improving livelihoods, the 1997–98 financial crisis caused the number of Indonesians living below the poverty line (measured in US dollar terms) to increase sharply (see Table 1) and then to stabilise.

Inflation, which continues to fluctuate today, has reduced the purchasing power of poor people throughout Indonesia. Poor families are squeezed by wages that do not keep up with inflation, while rents and prices (for power, water, cooking oil, basic foodstuffs, etc.) increase faster than inflation. As a consequence, average real incomes have fallen, creating greater problems for poor families striving to meet their basic needs.

Unemployment has increased steadily in recent years, from 4.9 per cent in 1996, 6.4 per cent in 1999, 8.1 per cent in 2001, to an estimated 9.7 per cent in 2004 (see Table 4, p.49). Equally important, the total number of unemployed people increased from 4.3 million in 1996 to an estimated 10.8 million in 2004. The number of underemployed with informal or part-time jobs is estimated at 32 million (Asian Labour News 2004). A principal driver of this trend is new entrants in the job market. In short, the Indonesian economy may be growing, but it is not creating sufficient jobs to absorb the increase in the workforce. Within these overall trends, the number of part-time workers in Indonesia has remained fairly constant over time.

The history of Unilever in Indonesia

The global Unilever business was founded in 1930, the product of the merger of Margarine Unie of the Netherlands and Lever Brothers of the UK. By 2003, Unilever was one of the leading companies in the manufacture and marketing of food, home, and personal-care products, with some 400 brands. A Fortune 500 multinational company with worldwide turnover of US$ 48.4 billion, Unilever has manufacturing operations in around 100 countries and sales in around 50 more, and it employs some 234,000 people.

Unilever Indonesia (UI) was established in 1933 with the founding of a local soap-manufacturing facility. In the 1930s the Indonesian soap market was estimated at 80,000 MT, 90 per cent of which was inexpensive, unbranded hard soaps. Most soaps were made by small-scale artisanal producers. The impact of UI's entry into the branded-soap market is unknown; but since its establishment, UI has shown its ability to become a leader in the branded-soap market, which had been dominated by Procter & Gamble and Colgate. By 1940, after only seven years in business, UI manufactured 12,000 MT of soap and was the largest soap producer in the country.

By 1948, UI had established or purchased factories to produce margarine, cosmetics, and edible oils. These activities grew until 1980, when all UI companies in Indonesia reorganised to form PT Unilever Indonesia. A year later, UI made the decision to go public on the Jakarta stock exchange (JSX) and sold 9.2 million shares locally (15 per cent of the total). The bulk of the equity value of the business (85 per cent) was retained by the parent company in the Netherlands.

Beginning in 1982, UI invested in a series of small to medium-sized enterprises (SMEs), to develop the capacity of third-party, partner companies to deliver according to UI standards – rather than build its own capacity or form joint ventures with larger domestic or multinational conglomerates. UI focused its support on four areas: distribution, raw-materials supply / packaging, warehousing / transportation, and production / manufacturing. In 1976 the company stopped using a Dutch-based trading house to distribute its products. Initially, it developed its own sales team; however, by 1982 it had established a network of Indonesian distributors, to whom it handed over sales activities. This sales force grew steadily to 385 distributors at the end of 2003. These companies now deliver UI brands to more than 550,000 shops weekly (UI management data).

These were sound business decisions. They lowered business costs and stabilised product supply by reducing UI's reliance on imported materials and reducing its vulnerability to foreign-exchange fluctuations. They also

Box 4: Seventy years of Unilever in Indonesia

Year	Event	Year	Event
1933	Soap factory opened	1984	Toilet-soap production moved from Colibri to Rungkut
1935	Margarine and vegetable-oil production begun		
1941	Colibri cosmetics factory opened	1990	UI acquired Sariwangi Tea
1942–46	Unilever control interrupted by World War II	1992	Wall's Ice Cream factory opened
1947	Facilities returned and reconditioned	1998	Acquired PT Yuhan HHC business
1947	Archa oil-milling factory opened	1999	Integration of PT Yuhan distribution with UI's system
1957	Unilever Indonesia nationalised; Unilever factories operated under government control	2000–01	Kimberly–Lever joint venture signed
			Acquired Bango Soy Sauce Business (joint venture with previous owner)
1967	Under new investment law, UI regained control of its factories		Integrated BestFoods business
1980	PT Unilever Indonesia restructured	2001-02	Joint venture with Texchem in mosquito coil business
1981	UI went public	2003–04	Acquired Taro Snacks business
1983	Personal-care products factory opened		Integrated PT Knorr (Best Foods) Indonesia

Source: Unilever Indonesia

reduced dependence on imported goods and foreign-owned distribution services. Equally important, these practices involved developing SMEs in Indonesia which have created significant multiplier effects (including innovation and new ways of doing business) within the local economy.

In 1996 UI sales increased by 20 per cent, while net earnings increased by 22 per cent over the previous year. UI invested US$ 153 million from 1991 to 1996 and US$ 117 million from 1997 to 2001.The company made a major investment in 1996–1997, building a new factory in Cikarang, and transferring operations from its site in Jakarta 30 kilometres away. According to UI officials, the new factory was more efficient, and the location allowed for easier access both to raw materials and to markets. Investments continued into 1998 to complete the construction, despite the economic crisis. As noted above, the cost of this work was funded from profits of UI, not by overseas investment. Today, UI is deeply integrated into the Indonesian economy. It sources and manufactures locally to sell to local consumers. It is not a company focused on exporting raw materials and manufactured goods to wealthy OECD country markets.[9]

In 2003, UI had more than 3,096 direct employees; nearly 25,000 people worked full time for UI within its network of direct partners; and hundreds of thousands of individuals worked within its value chain, from supplying raw materials to selling its brands. Virtually all management staff is Indonesian, as well as eight of ten UI board members. It is estimated that at least 95 per cent of Indonesians use one or more UI products every year, which indicates that approximately 90 per cent of poor people in Indonesia buy UI products every year.[10]

Assessing the impact of Unilever Indonesia

Foreign direct investment has the potential to make a significant impact on poor people, in both positive and negative ways, as listed below.

Potential positive and negative impacts of the local operations of an MNC

At the macro-economic level and through growth of the formal economy

- Providing financial resources for production or speculation (FDI or portfolio investment), in turn increasing or decreasing macro stability.
- Generating employment.
- Generating tax revenue.
- Supporting the growth of the formal economy.
- Creating or purchasing goods and services.
- Supplying technology and expertise.
- Encouraging or displacing or marginalising local producers.
- Influencing exchange rates.
- Contributing to balance-of-payments surplus or deficit.

Through direct interaction with people living in poverty

- Sourcing raw materials from poor communities.
- Producing products in poor communities and via SMEs.
- Supplying affordable, high-quality manufactured goods.
- Developing long-term predictable relationships with suppliers, small-scale distributors, and retailers.
- Expanding through innovation, or limiting choices for poor people through market dominance.
- Creating long supply chains which put pressure on those at the ends of the chain.
- Limiting or creating opportunities for poor people to participate throughout the value chain.
- Limiting or creating opportunities for poor people to develop new skills, or harness new technology and expertise.

Through influencing the business sector or government

- Providing competition in the marketplace.
- Extending internal policies and practices backwards and forwards through the value chain.
- Diffusing technology, expertise, and management skills.
- Influencing government policy, programmes, and practices on matters such as tax and labour legislation and product standards.
- Respecting or undermining local and international legislation and regulations.
- Operating in accordance with international standards, not lower ones.
- Creating benchmarks for good governance in local business community.
- Acting as a champion for corporate social responsibility with local and international businesses.

There are several ways to measure the impacts of an FMCG company in a country like Indonesia. This report has sought to focus on three of them. They are as follows.

- Identify all the different players in the value chain by following a product through the value chain from the production of raw-material inputs, through traders, processors, manufacturers, and distributors and retailers to the consumer who uses and disposes of its waste materials.
- Identify the number of jobs that are created at each level of the value chain as the product moves through it.
- Monitor the value of goods and services generated as products move through the value chain, and determine wages, prices, margins, mark-ups, and 'value' that are created and captured through the system.

It is possible to understand the implications for employment and value creation as products move from raw materials to consumer goods. More importantly, such analysis indicates the types of input or product that inherently generate more employment or value throughout the chain, and at specific points in the chain. It can also indicate where there are costs, risks, and opportunities associated with movement and transformation of products in the value chain. Through such analysis it is possible to identify key pressure points or bottlenecks which might also serve as leverage points for change in favour of poor people.

The structure of the report

The main text of this report is divided into five chapters, each of which considers a distinct aspect of UI's social and economic impacts. After setting out the research questions, data, and analysis, each chapter ends with a short section which describes key insights from the research.

Chapter 2 presents a broad assessment of UI's impacts at the macro-economic level in Indonesia. It provides data on UI's profits, shareholder payments, taxes, imports, and exports between 1999 and 2003. It also offers a brief case study of UI's business response during the Indonesian financial crisis of 1997–98.

Chapter 3 deals with UI's employment policies and practices. It shows the breakdown of the UI workforce into permanent, temporary, and contract employees, and gives data on the wages, benefits, and working conditions of each of these groups.

Recognising that the majority of those people who are linked to UI's operations are not direct employees, Chapter 4 presents an analysis of UI's impacts through its value chain. It considers UI's policies and practices through its production, supply, distribution, and retail chains. Because value-chain analysis is extremely complex, it was not possible to track the impact of all UI's products through the chain. One product – Kecap Bango sweet soy sauce, made from labour-intensive agricultural products – was selected to form the basis of an in-depth case study.

Chapter 5 considers UI's interactions with people on low incomes as consumers. It examines the extent to which UI's product content, packaging, pricing, and marketing make its products attractive to low-income consumers. It explores some key aspects of the debate concerning whether and under what conditions marketing goods to people living in poverty can be considered to have 'pro-poor' impacts.

The report recognises that the poverty impacts of a large company like UI may also occur through channels outside its business operations: for example, through its relationships with government or the business sector, and its wider links with communities. The research project did not explore these in depth. In order to round out the picture, however, Chapter 6 gives a brief description of some of UI's philanthropic activities and other community-based work, and UI's influence on the business community and government.

The final chapter offers a series of concluding reflections, from the perspectives of both Oxfam and Unilever, on the key overall lessons arising from the outcome and process of the research project. It includes a short section summarising comments on the report from the external reference group.

2 The impacts of Unilever Indonesia at the macro-economic level

At the level of the macro-economy, employment generation, strong public-sector investment, improved productivity, and macro-economic stability are among the foundations needed for economic development. Given the importance of these foundations, it is essential to understand the impacts of foreign direct investment within this context. For example, when, and to what extent, does foreign investment generate or reduce employment? Does it contribute to or reduce government revenue? In times of macro-economic instability, does foreign investment exacerbate or offset the crisis? This section of the report considers UI's performance in relation to some of these indicators. However, it is important to recognise that the activities of a single company have only limited impacts on national macro-economic indicators.

Set against the context of the 1997–98 Indonesian financial crisis, the effects of which were deeply felt in the Indonesian economy during much of the period under review, this chapter explores UI's economic performance, providing key financial data on profits, shareholder payments, taxes, imports, and exports for UI from 1999 to 2003. A brief analysis of UI's responses during the financial crisis also offers some important insights into how UI behaved at a particularly turbulent time.

Setting the context: the 1997–98 financial crisis

During the early 1990s, the Indonesian economy experienced annual GDP growth of 7–8 per cent, due to a large influx of foreign capital and improved relationships with the West (IMD 2001). Investments in the early 1990s supported growth and capacity expansion.

The financial crisis began in June 1997 when the Indonesian rupiah plunged in value, and many banks were forced to close. One in every five jobs in the country disappeared (*ibid.*). The private sector was immediately placed under great financial pressure, and many firms ceased trading because they could not cope with 80 per cent devaluation against the US dollar and a period of interest rates in excess of 100 per cent. Some international companies left Indonesia. Per capita GDP in Indonesia fell by 59 per cent in US$ terms, from US$ 1,140 in 1997 to US$ 470 in 1998 (Economist Intelligence Unit 2003) – and around 14 per cent in terms of real GDP per head. Average income per head did not return to 1996 levels until 2003 .

What had started as a monetary crisis quickly turned into a much more serious economic, social, and political crisis. In just two years, the levels of poverty in the country returned to those of the 1960s. Riots broke out in Jakarta in May 1998 and quickly spread to other regions of the country. President Suharto stepped down after 32 years of rule.

Over time, the Indonesian economy and political situation have stabilised. Consumer demand in the country has helped to sustain domestic economic activity since the onset of the crisis. The crisis provides the context for understanding Indonesia's experience of poverty during the period, as well as understanding UI's performance and its strategic decisions.

Unilever's organisation and recent performance in Indonesia

Figure 1 illustrates the structure of UI's business, from the supply of its raw materials, to sourcing, through UI production, to the marketplace. In 2003, UI directly employed 3,096 permanent employees and 184 temporary employees. A total of 1,989 contract workers was working on UI premises, hired and paid by third parties. UI operated the company's headquarters in Jakarta, and owned seven manufacturing plants and 17 sales offices and depots. One step removed from the core business, the company also had four dedicated third-party manufacturers and three co-packing facilities. UI dealt directly with 334 supplier companies, which source raw materials used in UI's products from a wide range of producers, including tens of thousands of farmers. UI brands reached the market through 385 direct distributors who, in turn, provided products to more than 1,267 sub-distributors. They, in turn, reached more than half a million retail shops directly. UI estimates that another one million outlets are supplied by other means.

Figure 1: UI and its business partners: structure of operations from sourcing to marketplace

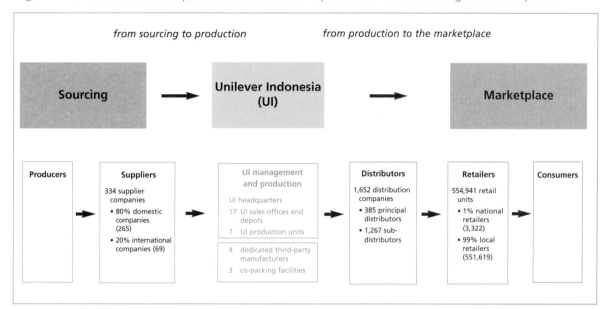

UI's financial performance

In 2001, UI was ranked by Asiaweek as the thirteenth-largest company (including parastatals[11]) by sales in Indonesia, and second in terms of profits as a percentage of sales. Only TELKOM, the Indonesian telecommunications company, reported higher profits. UI is the fourth-largest firm in the FMCG sector in Indonesia. The largest FMCG firm, Indofood Sukses Makmur, had a turnover more than double that of UI, and a domestic market capitalisation of US$ 2.04 bn. It is hard to compare UI's performance with that of other multinational companies such as Coca-Cola, Nestlé, Procter & Gamble, or Johnson & Johnson, because none of them is listed on the Jakarta Stock Exchange (JSX), so comparable data are not readily available.

On 31 December 2003, UI's price-to-earnings ratio[12] was 17.6, implying investor confidence in future growth and profits. UI's Indonesian shares out-performed the JSX from January 1999 through to December 2002. JSX shares increased in value on average 69 per cent over this four-year period, while UI's increased in value by 1,109 per cent.

In 2003, UI had a turnover of US$ 948 million. Of this total, 61.6 per cent of total sales were used for the ordinary operating expenses of the company: purchases, other expenditures, and labour; 17.9 per cent of total sales were paid to government in the form of taxes (not including sales tax); and 15.9 per cent of total sales were after-tax profits, of which one per cent was retained within the business for future investment, and 99 per cent were distributed as dividends to shareholders. This payout was exceptionally large. It was a special dividend by UI, intended to recognise the value of its shareholders on its seventieth anniversary of establishing operations in Indonesia. In 2003 the company also set aside approximately US$ 1 million for spending on community activities. On average, over the past five years, UI has paid out about 64 per cent of after-tax profits and retained some 36 per cent within the business, as Table 2 illustrates.

UI's overall performance in recent years was strongly affected by the country's financial crisis. It took until 2002 for UI's sales, in dollar terms, to return to 1996 levels. By 2003, UI had improved on all financial measures from 1996 (see Table 2). Sales, pre-tax profits, taxes paid, net profits, and shareholder payouts had all risen significantly, compared with 1996. In fact, UI had also improved its performance in two other key areas: the level of funds used for hedging had been reduced in absolute terms, and the volume of goods that it was importing from abroad had also declined, despite the fact in both cases that total sales had increased by nearly 28 per cent between 1996 and 2003.

Table 2: UI financial performance (1996 and 1999–2003)

Key indicators (US$ million)	1996	1999	2000	2001	2002	2003	Five-year average 1999-2003	Totals 1999–2003
Total sales	701	534	571	586	757	948	679	3396
Pre-tax profits	79	100	134	123	149	212	144	718
Total taxes paid[a]	118	108	120	115	136	170	130	649
Profits after corporate tax, comprising:	54	68	95	86	106	151	101	506
shareholder dividends	31	15	35	55	74	142	64	321
retained earnings	23	53	60	29	31	9	36	182

Source: Adapted from UI's Annual Report with additional data provided by UI

NB: Figures have been rounded to improve clarity, and the year 1996 has been included solely to indicate the level of business performance prior to the 1997–98 economic crisis: see Table 3 for data on currency fluctuations against the US dollar over this period.

[a] 'Total taxes paid' refers to all forms of taxes paid by UI (for example, employment taxes, local taxes, and payroll taxes) **excluding** sales taxes. The terms 'pre-tax profits' and 'profits after corporate tax' here refer to the inclusion or absence of corporate taxes only. See also Figure 2.

Figure 2: Distribution of UI's total pre-tax profits (1999–2003)

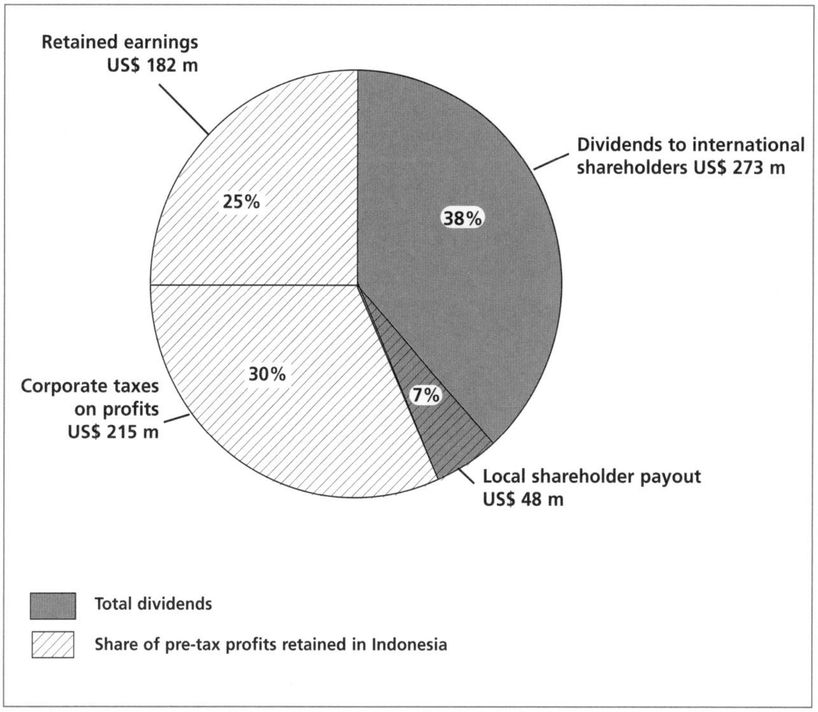

Source: UI Annual Reports, 1999-2003

Impact of UI's financial flows

Figure 2 demonstrates how UI's pre-tax profits have been distributed over the past five years. They are spread between dividends to shareholders (45 per cent of the total), retained earnings reinvested in the business in Indonesia (25 per cent), and corporate taxes paid to the government (30 per cent).

Between 1993 and the end of 2002, UI invested US$ 250 million in Indonesia. It plans to invest an additional US$ 500 million over the next ten years. UI paid a total of US$ 1,050 million in taxes between 1993 and 2002. According to data provided by UI and the Ministry of Finance, the company's proportion of Indonesia's total tax before and after 1998 reflects the acquisitions that the company made and suggests that the company's economic position recovered more quickly than that of other businesses. Prior to 1998, UI contributed around 0.43 per cent of government tax revenue; by 1999–2000, this share had almost doubled to 0.83 per cent.

In 2001, *CLSA Emerging Markets* ranked UI as the best investment in Indonesia (CLSA 2001). The article noted that UI had a growing cash reserve, and the issue would be whether to expand operations through acquisition or return the cash to shareholders (*ibid.*). UI annual reports from 2001 through 2003 indicate that the company did both. The highest marks given by CLSA to UI for corporate governance were in the following categories: social, fairness, discipline, and responsibility.

Figure 3: UI's international foreign-exchange, trade, and human-resource flows at a glance (2003)

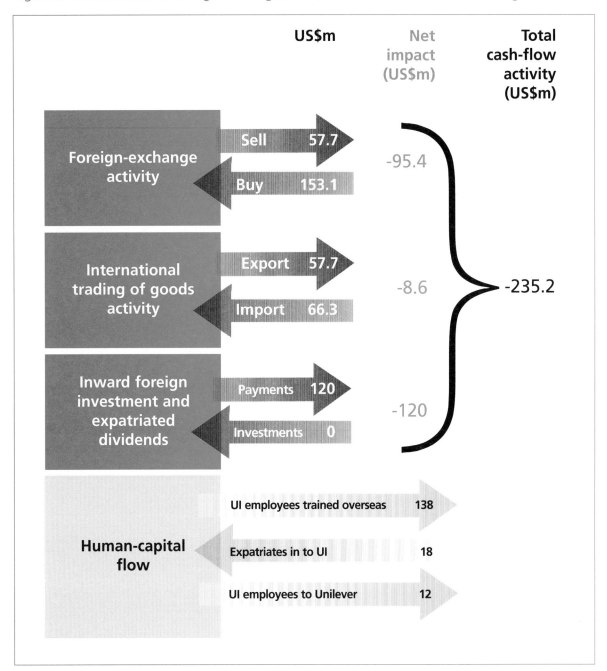

Source: UI internal data

Figure 3 identifies some of UI's net impacts in Indonesia in 2003. There was a net outflow of funds for foreign-exchange activity, importing goods for production, and dividends to foreign shareholders. In order to import raw materials and equipment that could not be bought or manufactured locally, as well as to buy dollar-denominated items in Indonesia and to meet its obligations to investors, UI is a net buyer of US dollars, as shown in Table 3.

The research for this report strongly suggests that the volume of trade from the buying and selling ratios indicates that the company does not hold currency or use financial hedging to speculate against the rupiah.[13] While economic impacts are of primary concern, it is interesting to note that in terms of human-capital flows, international companies are often criticised for giving more senior jobs to expatriates. In UI's case, expatriates hold fewer than 5 per cent of senior management positions, even though at this time there are more expatriates entering the country to work in UI than there are Indonesians working abroad for Unilever, the parent company (see Figure 3). In the case of UI, these expatriates are as likely to be from Singapore, Philippines, India, Hong Kong, or South Africa as they are from Europe or the USA.

Table 3: Exchange-rate fluctuations and UI's currency transactions (1996–2003)

UI exchange transaction (US$ million)	1996	1997	1998	1999	2000	2001	2002	2003
Rp to $ exchange rate (annual average)	2,347	2,952	9,875	7,809	8,534	10,266	9,261	8,571
Foreign-exchange buying	127	111	57	86	91	96	124	153
Foreign-exchange selling	11	8	8	26	30	30	48	58
Net foreign-exchange impact	-115	-103	-49	-60	-61	-65	-77	-95

Source: UI internal data

In terms of purchasing locally rather importing, both the volume and the value of UI's imported and dollar-denominated raw-material purchases increased after the financial crisis. Of UI's foreign-exchange purchases, worth US$ 153.1 million, US$ 103 million were for local and international inputs used to manufacture products (US$ 66 million for imported inputs, and US$ 38 million for products purchased in Indonesia that had to be paid for in US dollars, such as products like palm oil which could have otherwise been exported for dollars). A total of US$ 9.19 million was used to purchase equipment and fixed assets. UI's policy on fixed assets has shifted to one of making local purchases whenever possible. For example, in 2003 the company spent US$ 26.9 million on locally manufactured equipment, and several local engineering firms were encouraged to produce equipment for UI for the first time. This saved money for UI, because the equipment was up to 60 per cent cheaper than foreign-bought equivalents, and the move boosted the local manufacturing sector's jobs and technical capacity.

In 2003, UI exported 33,523 MT of product, worth US$ 57.69 million. This represented 6.4 per cent of total sales by volume. UI exports finished products such as margarine, black tea, ice cream, edible products, toothpaste, skin creams, deodorant, toilet soaps, and detergent powder to 18 countries, with Australia and Malaysia importing the largest volume and value of products. In addition, UI exports crude and refined glycerine.

UI's response to the financial crisis

Given the severity of the financial crisis, many Indonesians, including UI's local stakeholders, are concerned about how business, and international companies in particular, behaved in the crisis, and how they have rebuilt their businesses since then. UI describes six specific factors that helped it to respond to the crisis, while maintaining the company's basic values and relations with consumers, employees, and suppliers. They were the following.

Consumer access

UI recognised during the crisis that if consumers could not afford to buy its products, the company would not stay in business. It pursued three separate strategies to address this problem. It expanded the number of its popular products that were available in affordable sachets. Secondly, it created new, less expensive formulations of popular products. And thirdly, where possible, it substituted locally sourced ingredients for more expensive imported ones, to reduce the price of known brands. The company maintained its policy of making its products available to distributors at the same price throughout the country. These strategies enabled UI not only to maintain its consumer base, but actually to increase it in many areas.

Employee numbers

UI records show that the number of permanent employees increased throughout the financial crisis. The company gave a high priority to retaining workers, even though many other companies were closing or reducing operations and laying off workers.

UI staff provided management with information on the crisis, as well as ideas for how to address it. Employees were encouraged to think about the likely impacts of economic developments on the company, and how it should respond. Staff suggested ideas that succeeded in reversing sales declines of 50 per cent or more in several categories during the onset of the crisis. In all, more than 200 constructive suggestions were received by the company over one two-week period (IMD 2001).

Relationships with partner companies

UI's strategy was to focus on the business essentials and work through the financial crisis, but it could not do this alone. UI brought suppliers, manufacturers, and distributors together and re-negotiated margins throughout the value chain, so that products could reach consumers at prices that would be more affordable, and the companies in the whole chain could remain in business. While this strategy did not improve anyone's margins, it did allow margins to become more transparent and companies to remain in business that might otherwise have failed. UI and its partners recognised that all would lose if consumers could not afford their products. In the end, this strategy enabled the companies to survive the crisis.

Brand acquisition and strategic joint ventures

During the financial crisis, UI bought strategic local brands and created joint ventures with companies that continued to manufacture on contract. For example, brands of PT Yuhan (fabric softener) were acquired, and a joint venture was created with PT Anugrah Setia Lestari (former owner of Bango Brands) to manage the production of Kecap Bango. These actions undoubtedly sustained the economic activity of some of these companies, but some have lost their independence because ownership moved, in whole or in part, to UI.

Currency transactions

UI maintained a conservative foreign-exchange policy on currency markets through hedging (buying and holding more stable currencies, such as US dollars, to protect funds against the fall in local currency values) to the extent necessary to minimise risk during the financial crisis. Some 62 per cent of dollar buys were used to purchase raw materials (both imports and dollar-denominated commodities within Indonesia) such as palm oil, imported chemicals, or manufactured inputs. Some of UI's local suppliers depended on foreign inputs, so all their transactions with UI were dollar-based. In addition, hedging allowed the company to obtain sufficient foreign exchange to maintain its products' price stability. In short, the company bought currency but did not make currency speculation a new 'business line'. During this period the company also adopted a policy of holding large amounts of cash, to guarantee timely payment to employees and suppliers during periods of uncertainty. The company's foreign-exchange buying activity had no impact on the value of the rupiah against the US dollar, in part because UI is too small to influence the currency (see Table 3).

Focus on the local market

UI did not use the low rupiah production costs in Indonesia to sell abroad to earn foreign exchange. Instead, UI and its suppliers began to purchase more ingredients locally and to focus on expanding the domestic market. While exports might have helped UI's profit and loss account (as well as Indonesia's), it was assumed that the economy would eventually turn around, creating a volume of manufacturing in Indonesia which could not be sustained over time, as local costs increased again relative to international markets.

UI's strategy during the financial crisis was influenced by what other Unilever companies around the world had learned when facing hyperinflation in their local economies. It quickly paid off. By 1999, UI had a record performance, with after-tax profits of Rp 533 billion (US$ 68 million) and in 2000 after-tax profits of Rp 813 billion (US$ 95 million). UI 'became a market leader in the fast-moving consumer goods industry with sales of over Rp 4,870 billion (US$ 571 million) in 2000' (IMD 2001). Furthermore, by 2000, UI was operating seven factories to produce consumer products in 14 categories. It has been able to expand and succeed when many other firms have ceased to trade.

Given the special circumstances of the 1997–98 financial crisis, it is interesting to evaluate UI's performance relative to that of other FMCG companies, and to compare sales between the crisis years and the present. Between 1998 and 2002, sales in Indonesia's FMCG market fell by nearly 22 per cent. Sales of Indonesia's largest FMCG company, Indofood Sukses Makmur, declined by nearly half, from US$ 1.77 billion to $0.9 billion. By comparison, UI's sales for the period more than doubled, growing by 137 per cent from US$ 319 million to $757 million.

The macro-economic financial crisis created rapid inflation; but, beginning in 1997, UI aggregate product prices and the Indonesian consumer price index (CPI) began to deviate. UI's price increases began showing slower growth rates than for the CPI as a whole. For example, in 1998, UI prices in general rose at a rate of only 92.6 per cent of inflation as measured by CPI; in 1999 the rate was 80 per cent, in 2000 84.4 per cent, and in 2001 84.1 per cent. This indicates that UI was able to deliver its products to consumers at prices below the overall rate of inflation. (It is not possible to say how this compares with other local or international companies and goods in the same sector.)

Key insights: the impacts of Unilever Indonesia at the macro-economic level

A company's business model is an important determinant of how, and to what extent, it can contribute at the macro-economic level to a country's poverty-reduction efforts. There are many different types of business model among MNCs. This research found that UI is deeply embedded in Indonesia's economy. It contributes directly to the country's tax base and employment. In addition, a 'map' of UI's operations shows an extensive and linked set of suppliers and distributors who also contribute to the tax base and employment. Moreover, it is in the backward linkages to suppliers, and forward linkages to retailing, that large numbers of people living in poverty are interacting with the company value chain, as producers of agricultural raw materials, as workers in small shops, and as consumers.

Unilever Indonesia flourished despite the financial crisis that began in 1997, by adapting its business. This involved expanding sales of products in smaller packages that consumers could afford; switching to local sources of materials in response to the devaluation (which had made imports much more expensive); and buying local companies affected by the crisis. In terms of social impact, this was largely a 'win–win' response to the crisis.

The company expanded its operations in the country, and increased its backward and forward linkages in the economy. As a consequence, it emerged as an even more profitable company, at a time when the climate for economic activity was very difficult, many other MNCs were withdrawing from the country, and poverty was increasing.

The majority of revenues generated by UI remains in the country through local sourcing, wages, taxes to government, and, to a lesser extent, dividends to local shareholders. Nevertheless, overall UI's direct operations represent a net outflow of cash, because of import purchases and dividend payments to shareholders abroad.

Clearly, governments, CSOs, and companies themselves could do more to enhance the contribution of business to poverty reduction if positive and negative impacts on the local economy were better understood, documented, and used to inform policy making. Transparency of financial and management information by companies is an important contribution to this process.

3 The employment impacts of Unilever Indonesia

Through their local operations, Unilever and other large MNCs can have a significant impact on employment and employment conditions in countries like Indonesia. UI's activities are important not only because of its size, but also because of its investment in both production and distribution, and the depth to which its business activities reach into the local economy. In terms of employment, UI interacts with people who are its employees, workers in companies within UI's value chain, primary producers of agricultural products that are processed into the products that UI sells, and sellers of UI's products.

Assessing the impact of employment on poverty is more than a matter of determining how many people are employed and at what levels. Although that is an important first step, the assessment also requires ascertaining whether people, through their employment, are able to gain skills, build economic security, accumulate assets, and make sustainable improvements in their lives. Moreover, the policies and practices of MNCs are important not only for their direct employees, but also for those working in other businesses throughout their value chain, and for the positive or negative influence that the MNCs may have on the employment situation more broadly in the country.

This research explored employment issues in three main areas. First, it examined the principles, values, and policies on which UI bases its approach to doing business. Second, it explored the extent to which UI takes responsibility for maintaining its standards among its own employees and its contractors. Third, it attempted to assess the extent to which UI's policies and practices have benefited people or have had negative consequences.

Employment in Indonesia

About half of the population of Indonesia lives in poverty. This includes poor agricultural workers who are self-employed on their farms or working for others, as well as wage workers who are engaged in the formal or informal economy. Most employment in Indonesia is in the latter rather than the former sector. The 1970s and 1980s saw large increases in the number of workers in the formal economy, and more specifically in manufacturing, including a large increase in the number of young women workers. From 1986 to 1999, the proportion of the urban labour force that lived in cities increased from 23.6 per cent to 38.1 per cent (SMERU 2001) and to 40.3 per cent by 2002 (Economist Intelligence Unit 2003).

Table 4: Employment in Indonesia (1996–2004)

Period	Economic growth (%)	New employment created (million)	New entrants to workforce (million)	Total unemployed (million)	Unemployed as % of total workforce %
1996	7.8	1.9	2.3	4.3	4.9
1998	-13.3	2.2	3.1	5.0	5.5
1999	0.79	1.5	2.5	6.0	6.4
2000	4.9	1.0	0.9	5.8	6.0
2001	3.8	0.9	3.1	8.0	8.1
2002	4.3	0.8	2.0	9.1	9.1
2003	4.5	-0.8	-0.5	9.5	9.5
2004	4.8	1.5	1.9	9.9	9.7

Notes:

Data for years 1996, 1999, 2000, 2001, 2002 and 2003 were sourced from Indonesia's National Labour Force Survey (SAKERNAS, BPS).

Data for 2000 exclude Maluku province.

Data for years 2001, 2002 and 2003 use new definition of revised open unemployment, and include Maluku province.

Data for 2004 were projected by Indonesia's Central Planning Agency (BAPPENAS).

Source: Widianto / BAPPENAS, 2003

While the number of part-time workers in Indonesia has remained fairly constant over time, Table 4 shows that the unemployment rate has increased steadily over the past decade, both before and after the financial crisis. The consequences of the economic crisis in Indonesia for employment have been profound. The unemployment rate increased steadily from 4.9 per cent in 1996 to 9.7 per cent in 2004. Equally important, the absolute number of unemployed people increased from 4.3 million in 1996 to an estimated 9.9 million in 2004, with new entrants in the job market exceeding the number of jobs being created in every year but 2000. With no social-security provisions, the unemployed are forced to take whatever work they can find, and therefore they are in a weak bargaining position and are more vulnerable to exploitation. Research suggests that the consequences of the economic crisis in Indonesia for employment have been profound, and job retrenchment after the crisis affected women more than men (ILO 1999).

Unionisation of the workforce has been a highly contested issue over the last few decades. Unionisation levels are relatively high, at about 9 per cent of the total labour force and about 25 per cent of the labour force in the formal economy (Friedrich Ebert Stiftung 2004). Previously the government recognised only one trade union, the All Indonesia Labour Union (SPSI), which was closely associated with the government during the Suharto period. In 1994 a Ministerial Decree allowed formation of independent trade unions at the plant level. In 1998, at the end of the Suharto period, new regulations on trade unions ended the effective monopoly of SPSI on union activity at the national level. Law No. 21/2000 on trade unions came into force in 2000, recognising trade-union rights such as collective bargaining, the right to represent membership in disputes, and the right to strike (only after intensive mediation efforts and after giving a warning of an impending strike).

Currently there are more than 60 trade unions operating at the national level, and at the plant level there are more than 18,000 (Friedrich Ebert Stiftung 2004). But the existence of many trade unions does not mean that the collective bargaining process has worked. Companies tend to talk with the main formal trade union (SPSI), rather than with more independent unions created by workers, which often have limited capacity or leadership. Each year there are hundreds of strikes and lock-outs, and according to several sources there are many cases where workers are dismissed after strikes, contrary to legal protections. Moreover, the increase in outsourcing has reduced the extent to which trade unions are able to organise and recruit members among workers, and solidarity between workers is thus undermined.[14]

For the economy as a whole, the proportion of workers in the formal economy who receive less than the minimum wage declined from a peak in 1995 of just over 21 per cent of workers to just over 10 per cent in 2000. The domestic food and beverage sector is known for underpaying its workers. In a survey undertaken by SMERU (2001), researchers found that in this sector an estimated 40 per cent of workers were paid below the minimum wage in the formal economy, while 68 per cent were paid below the minimum wage in the informal economy. So while fewer people are paid the minimum wage in the informal economy, the formal economy is still not meeting its obligations.

In addition, the ways in which companies calculate and comply with minimum-wage regulations in Indonesia vary enormously: minimum wages are set at sub-national levels, making comparison and monitoring more difficult. Large firms in Indonesia usually interpret minimum wages as applying only to the basic wage that their workers receive, while allowances—both fixed and variable—are not included as part of the minimum wage but are added on. By contrast, medium-sized and small firms mostly interpret minimum wages (and their compliance with them) as applying to the whole worker-benefit package, which may include transportation allowances or other benefits as well as overtime pay.

In Indonesia, as elsewhere, contract work (whereby workers are employed through labour contracts with external firms) is an increasingly common feature of the labour market. Oxfam has argued that this trend leads to an increase in the number of young workers, particularly women, working in precarious conditions, with no guarantee of job security, union representation, a decent wage, sickness leave, maternity leave, or health care.

UI's employment impacts

Employment linked to UI's operations takes a number of different forms, and includes six categories of people who make at least part of their livelihood from UI's 'value chain'. They are the following:

- permanent employees
- temporary employees: skilled workers hired directly by UI to fill temporary employment gaps
- contract workers: workers hired through contractors to perform unskilled jobs
- employees and contract workers of companies who supply materials and services to UI
- people in distribution or retail shops or who are self-employed in UI's distribution chain
- producers and waged workers who grow or collect the raw materials that are sold as ingredients for finished products.

The first three categories of worker perform their duties on UI property. This section examines UI's relationship with these three categories of worker. The other categories are discussed in the sections on supply and distribution in Chapter 4.

The UI workforce

In 2003, UI had 3,096 direct employees, of whom 184 were temporary employees, and 1,989 contract workers. A review of company-provided information covering the period 1996–2003 (shown in Table 5) gives a snapshot of the employment profile. The number of permanent employees increased, but it became a smaller proportion of the total workforce of UI. The number and proportion of contract workers increased considerably between 2002 and 2003 to meet business needs during this time. UI did not collect comparable data on contract workers prior to 2002.

The closer and more formally employees are linked to UI's operations, the more they benefit directly from the company. Permanent and temporary employees generally have higher incomes and benefits than contract workers who are not hired directly by UI.

Table 5: UI employment data by type (1996–2003)

	1996	1997	1998	1999	2000	2001	2002	2003
Total employees, of whom	1,972	2,046	2,126	2, 180	2,352	2,895	3,011	3,096
temporary employees	112	122	48	90	231	515	244	184
Total contract workers	——	——	——	——	——	——	1,423	1,989

Source: UI

UI hires both permanent and temporary employees directly. Temporary employees are generally skilled workers who are hired on one-year contracts to fill job openings. They are hired as temporary employees, but may sometimes become permanent employees.

The third category of worker consists of skilled, semi-skilled, or unskilled contract workers (such as gardeners, cleaners, loaders/unloaders) who are hired and paid by third-party contractor agencies, and most of whom work on UI premises.[15] UI pays the contracting company for a service, and these people are employed by the contractor to perform it. A small proportion of these individuals fulfil UI's criteria for employment and eventually become direct employees.

Permanent employees

According to UI's written employment policies, the company has systems in place to recruit, train, and promote permanent employees according to their qualifications and abilities. The data provided by UI and corroborated by this project's research team support the view that the company does not discriminate against candidates on the grounds of sex, religion, or ethnicity.

About 70 per cent of workers are male – a figure that is somewhat higher than the national average of 61–62 per cent. But a higher proportion of UI's female workers, compared with males, is reportedly promoted. About 92 per cent of UI's workforce is Muslim (compared with the national average of 88 per cent), but no information is available on ethnic minorities. Two-thirds of all employees have had a high-school education, while nearly 30 per cent have higher degrees. High education levels are an indication of the level of competition for positions at UI.

UI reports a low rate of employee turnover, with less than one per cent of its employees dismissed each year, and approximately 5 per cent leaving (most retiring) annually. The vast majority of UI permanent employees work for 20 years or more for the company, and stay in employment until they retire.[16]

According to UI officials, other key policies for *permanent* employees include the following:

- **Contracts**. All workers have a written contract. No worker contracts are broken unless a product line is discontinued. When that happens, it is UI's policy to make every effort to find another position in the company for the affected workers.

- **Benefits.** Health-care allowance is provided to all employees and their families (including the costs of medical consultations, eyeglasses, hospitalisation, medicines, counselling, and child care). Sick employees are visited by HR department officials, and information is provided to them and their families about their benefits. Maternity leave is provided in accordance with the law. Employees also have access to fitness facilities.

- **Retirement.** Two years before retirement, a worker is given guidance and counselling to prepare for retirement, and assistance with opening a business should he or she desire to do so. Health-care costs are reimbursed for up to one year after retirement.

- **Pensions.** All UI employees are part of the company's pension plan. Unlike most workers in Indonesia, all UI permanent employees have access to a company pension fund. In 1992, the government extended the retirement age from 55 to 60 years of age, as part of new regulations on pension funds.

The research for this report also investigated how company employment policies were implemented in practice. UI reports that its employment procedures match or exceed Indonesian legal requirements. Research conducted for this report found that the youngest worker was 20 years old (18 is the minimum legal age).

Workers' right to choose which union to join and to represent their interests has been guaranteed by law in Indonesia since 2000. Unilever's global policy is to fully respect the right of employees to join trade unions where they wish, and to work with unions when they are formed and formally recognised as negotiation partners.[17] According to UI, company workers have the right to belong to any union in Indonesia. In practice, all of UI's non-management permanent employees belong to SPSI, the trade union described above. UI maintains that SPSI works effectively on behalf of, and has the confidence of, its employees. In the research done for this report, all of the UI employees interviewed said that they were union members, but none held office. There is a two-year Collective Labour Agreement negotiated between the union and the company, and three-monthly meetings to deal with issues arising. Those interviewed by the research team felt that UI did not try to influence SPSI. On the other hand, Oxfam in Indonesia questions whether SPSI may constrain freedom of association by preventing workers from becoming members of other trade unions, and whether SPSI can represent workers' best interests.

The proportion of UI expenditures for labour from 1996 to 2002 was relatively flat, at 5.6 per cent of total spending, although it had increased to 7 per cent in 2003. This indicates that before, during, and after the financial crisis wages neither substantially increased nor decreased relative to other expenses. Generally speaking, UI is positioned in the top quartile of all Indonesian companies for pay and benefits. Table 6 shows UI entry-level salaries compared with minimum wages in Jakarta (1996–2003).

Table 6: UI monthly salaries compared with Indonesian minimum wage (1996–2003)

	1996	1997	1998	1999	2000	2001	2002	2003
Entry-level salary (1,000 Rp)	195.0	204.4	326.0	352.6	481.3	645.8	698.4	777.2
Minimum wage in Jakarta	156.0	172.5	198.5	230.0	286.0	426.3	591.0	631.6
UI salary as % of minimum wage	125	118	164	153	168	151	118	123

Source: UI

The lowest-paid employee in UI is an entry level in 'job class' 4. As Table 6 shows, such a new employee receives a basic salary that is 20 per cent more than the minimum wage. Even ignoring the free medical insurance for each employee's family, when additional benefits are factored in UI actually spends 2.4 times more than required by law. This expenditure includes an annual allowance, home allowance, leave allowance, product allowance, and meal allowance, which take the entry-level employee's total wages and benefits package to a figure of 1,538,234 Rp (US$ 179.50).

However, it could be argued that the minimum wage is not in fact a good comparator, given concerns about whether it is sufficient. For example, in 2003 the Indonesian government set the minimum monthly wage (for Java) at Rp 631,554 (US$ 74). This sum is considered to be equal to 90 per cent of the value of 'minimum livelihood needs' (KHM, described in Chapter 1) for one person, not for the typical worker who is supporting several members of a household. The government set the legal minimum wage below the KHM in an attempt to encourage the creation of more jobs.

Many CSOs, including Oxfam, have called on governments and companies to adopt the concept of a 'living wage'. There is not full international agreement on how to define a living wage. ILO Convention 131 on fixing a minimum wage does not explicitly call for a living wage, but requires that elements considered in fixing minimum wages should include, in addition to economic factors and national conditions, 'the needs of workers and their families, taking into account the general level of wages in the country, the cost of living, social security benefits, and the relative living standards of other social groups'.

Table 7: UI average monthly earnings of entry-level permanent employees (Java), (2003)

Pay and benefits	UI payment (Rp)	Indonesian minimum wage (Rp)
Minimum salary	777,183	631,554
Annual allowance	93,441	-
Home allowance	185,000	-
Leave allowance	62,274	-
Product allowance	145,336	-
Meal allowance	275,000	-
TOTAL	1,538,234 (US$179.50)	631,554 (US$74)

Source: UI

Against this background, UI's average payment for wages and allowances for lowest entry-level permanent employees is more than twice the monthly KHM.

UI managers identify open communications, skills training, and concern for health and safety as being among the reasons why people work for UI. Performance in these areas is backed by company data:

- **Openness**. UI appears to have transparent and on-going communication with employees. The company reports that in the last ten years no legal actions have been taken against the company by employees.

- **Skills training.** All employees receive at least some training every year. UI aims to invest in training for employees, to help them to develop skills that they can retain and use whether inside or outside UI. In 2003, 2,620 workers received personal performance appraisals.

- **Health and safety.** UI has high health and safety standards. According to UI data, only four accidents occurred between 1998 and 2003 that required employees to miss work. An additional eight accidents occurred over the same six-year period, but the individuals concerned were able to continue work. No entry-level employees were involved in accidents at UI between 1998 and 2003. As part of its Total Productive Maintenance (TPM) management, UI's health and safety reports are externally audited by the Japan Institute of Productive Maintenance. UI received the Indonesian government's 'Zero Accident Award' for ten consecutive years between 1992 and 2002. The research for this report found that when individuals are found not to be using protective gear, workers (and their supervisors) are given written warnings. After three warnings, a formal dismissal process is begun. UI's working conditions are pegged to Unilever's international standards.

Unilever Indonesia is one of Unilever's many operating companies around the world, and as such it manages its business within a common framework of values set by the company's Corporate Purpose (www.unilever.com/company/ourpurpose/) and its Code of Business Principles (www.unilever.com/company/ourprinciples/). UI is supported by a range of policies on issues as diverse as employment practices, relations with business partners, and the management of health, safety, and the environment. One benefit of this arrangement is that the local company's policy and practice are set to meet high international standards, as well as local legal and other requirements. In addition, because UI is listed on the local stock exchange, the level of public disclosure required is higher than that for unlisted companies. This has led to a regular and detailed annual publishing of information, not solely on financial performance but also on wider matters. The company's reporting has led in turn to regular reports by independent financial analysts, and these reports are a good source of information about the company.

Unilever's approach to incorporating its stated corporate values and written policies into the practices of its business in different countries and cultures around the world is through self-assessment and positive-assurance systems to monitor overall operation of policies and practices. Performance is also subject to regular review by internal auditors, as well as regional and international auditors, consisting of senior managers from sister companies within the Unilever family. In addition, UI has an independent Board of Commissioners, which receives regular reports from the company's Board of Directors, its Audit Committee, and its external auditors (PricewaterhouseCoopers) on business performance and integrity. They issue a comment on the company's performance each year in the annual report.

Contract workers

Many companies and organisations around the world are increasingly using contracted and sub-contracted labour, both on and off their premises. The tasks range from cleaning by a sub-contractor, to temporary office work contracted through employment agencies, to outsourcing complete production operations performed by hundreds of employees. Employers use contract labour because it offers them flexibility, allowing them to focus on 'core competencies' rather than having many specialisations, to reduce or spread risks, and to reduce total employment costs.

Research[18] suggests that women are particularly likely to be engaged in contract work in factories and the processing activities of supply chains, and that they experience lower levels of job security, pay, and benefits than either male contract workers or permanent employees. Moreover, 'flexibility' of workers often means no benefits and, as documented by research in supply chains worldwide, it can mean that people have to work in multiple flexible jobs in order to feed their families and pay health-care costs that are not covered by employers.

In 2000 the Indonesian government introduced new legislation, giving companies more freedom to outsource operations, and limiting protection of workers. Following criticisms of this trend by workers and labour groups within Indonesia, the government has prepared a new decree with tighter regulations on outsourcing.[19] The new decree allows companies to subcontract to other companies certain jobs that are not included in their core business. Outsourcing companies are no longer allowed to operate rolling contracts past the legal time limit, and are required to recruit and employ workers on a permanent basis.

In 2003 the total number of contract workers working for UI was 1,989, representing nearly 38 per cent of all labour working directly in UI facilities. In 2003 the number of contract labourers increased by more than seven per cent as a proportion of all labour working on UI premises, while the total of permanent employees increased by only two per cent. This was because there was a temporary increase in contract workers to handle the move of hair-care operations from Surabaya to Jakarta, and the need to package tea on manual assembly lines, pending the delivery of new equipment.

UI contracts workers through 21 agencies. These workers are typically employed in cleaning, gardening, catering, and loading products; they work in 17 sales depots and warehouses, in addition to seven manufacturing plants located in Surabaya and Bekasi/Jakarta.

For UI, contract workers are an important element of its overall human resources strategy. The company aims to ensure that each individual adds value in his or her role. The need for contract workers will change over time with seasonal variations, changing technology, and competitor and market developments. Against this background UI takes into consideration, as requested by the government and in line with its CSR policies, ways in which it might generate rather than reduce employment, particularly among low-skilled workers within its contracted workforce.

UI policy requires all agencies providing contract labour services to the company to obey the law – including honouring the agreed length of employment contracts. UI annually checks/audits its 21 contractor agencies against the terms of their contracts, including adherence to its Code of Business Principles, licences, and observance of manpower laws and health and safety laws. UI as a large company also withholds tax for payment by the contractor, as required by government. For UI, it is in the company's interest that the contractor company obeys the law. Where breaches are reported, UI will act with the contractor to correct them. According to data supplied by UI, the company's contract workers receive remuneration more than 20 per cent better than that required under Indonesian law or often given by other companies. Basic training is provided by the contractor/agencies, and UI provides additional training for contract workers in safety, hygiene, and fire-fighting.

Research for this report illustrated some of the problems that may arise. In interviews with 22 contract workers (including drivers, maintenance workers, secretaries, and packers), 13 reported that they had been retained as contract workers beyond the legal three-year period of time (one had worked for ten years on contract) after which they should have become permanent employees. The fear of losing their jobs meant that most never made complaints to their employer (the companies who supply contract workers to UI). UI was surprised by this reported finding and undertook to conduct a specific review of contract workers' employment-contract status with the agencies.

UI does not hold gender-disaggregated data on contract workers, but obviously some proportion of them is female. Many of those interviewed in this research said that female contract workers fear dismissal for complaining, for being ill, or missing work. One woman contract worker interviewed for this research project feared getting pregnant because she believed she would lose her job with her employer, the contracting agency. UI and other companies need to respond to this type of gender discrimination and find ways to remove it. There is a range of ways in which corporate policies and practices for permanent employees could be encouraged among the labour-supplier companies with whom UI works. UI acknowledges this point. Where under-performance on any of the parameters of its contracts is noted, UI will act with the contractor to correct this.

The use of contract labour is a global trend. In 2003 its use increased on UI premises for specific purposes. While future trends in contract employment at UI are unclear, Oxfam is concerned that the number of contract workers functioning within UI is significant, at around 40 per cent of the workforce in 2003. Oxfam research in this and other business sectors has found that global companies can have a positive influence on the wages and conditions of contract workers. While contracting services is a legal practice and may meet the needs of companies, Oxfam fears that it may also allow companies to avoid the direct costs of hiring permanent employees. Companies have a duty to ensure that the contracted companies obey the law and uphold labour standards. The challenge for companies like UI is to find effective ways of monitoring the standards of operations that are outside their direct influence.

For governments and CSOs, the long-term wider challenge related to contract work is to ensure the enforcement of good labour standards, to combat exploitative labour arrangements, and to support meaningful bargaining power of workers in the economy generally. Whether contract workers are on the first step of a corporate ladder, or whether they are working in precarious conditions with little chance of upward mobility, depends considerably on the practices of the companies involved and the extent to which economic opportunities are available and dispersed throughout the economy. This issue is explored in the next chapter, which attempts to quantify the value and employment supported by UI operations in Indonesia.

Key insights: UI's employment impacts

The research supporting this report, albeit limited, suggests that UI sets high standards for the treatment of its permanent employees, in line with the global Unilever Code of Business Principles. Pay and benefits are above what is required by law, positioning UI in the top quartile of Indonesian companies. In terms of policy and practice, there are high health and safety standards, good retirement and maternity benefits and workplace facilities, and a strong emphasis on training. All UI employees have a written contract, and there are clear procedures for negotiations between workers, the union, and management.

Research for this project suggests that the closer and more formally employees are linked to UI's operations, the more they benefit directly from the company. Contract workers generally had lower pay and benefits than UI's permanent employees, and different contractual conditions. Although contract employment is recognised as an important part of UI's business strategy, the research indicates two respects in which improvement is needed, and UI is committed to take action accordingly to protect labour rights. These two areas for improvement are (1) ensuring that UI's labour-supply companies observe legal requirements concerning the transfer of temporary employees to permanent employment contracts; and (2) the need to respond to concerns raised by a female contract worker that illness or pregnancy could result in loss of employment.

The research illustrated how contracting out employment may reduce a parent company's ability to monitor the situation of contract workers or suppliers' employees – a fact which, in Oxfam's view, may result in the emergence of gaps between corporate policy and practice in the treatment of contracted workforce. This structural weakening of the relationship between employers and their workers can be exacerbated by contract workers' difficulties in joining unions. For these reasons, companies, governments, and CSOs need to work together to protect the rights of contract workers. Given the rapid expansion of contract labour globally, there is a need for a much better understanding of how contracting operates, and how workers' rights can be protected.

4 The value chain from supply to distribution

The business operations of a large company like UI are at the centre of a complex value chain with both forward and backward linkages into the economy. The company relates most directly and most often with those companies that work closest to it in the value chain (for example, direct suppliers and distributors of its products), and more distantly with those entities that are farthest from it and with whom it has the least contact (for instance, agricultural producers on the supply side, and small-scale retailers on the distribution side).

This chapter aims to assess the extent to which the producers, suppliers, distributors, and retailers who are linked to UI through its value chain are able to participate in the benefits of UI's successes. It looks first at UI's relationships with its direct supplier companies, then analyses the benefits and risks to producers of raw materials arising from their participation in the UI value chain. Next it considers the impacts of involvement at the distribution and retail end of the UI value chain. Finally, it analyses and compares the creation of value and the distribution of income for the different actors in UI's value chain as a whole, as products move from the materials stage, through the supply stage, to distribution.

The creation of value, income, assets, and employment in itself is not necessarily an indicator of impacts that benefit poor people. Whether or not benefits accrue to people living in poverty also depends on the way in which the benefits of value-chain participation are distributed. Therefore the analysis addresses the question of how becoming part of the UI value chain affects the lives of people living in poverty in Indonesia, and how these impacts could benefit poor people further.

UI manufactures and markets hundreds of products. Production volumes are dominated by its home-care and personal-care brands (84 per cent of sales in 2003), with ingredients that come mainly from highly processed inputs and industrial processes, with smaller inputs of agricultural raw materials. Value-chain analysis is extremely complex. It is virtually impossible, given real constraints of time and money, to undertake a complete value-chain analysis of all UI products and investments. In addition, the impacts are dynamic and challenging to measure, so that understanding what is happening at one point does not necessarily hold constant as industry operating practices evolve. This report considers value-chain analysis broadly across the business and then looks in depth at one of UI's food brands: *kecap bango*, a sweet soy sauce made from labour-intensive agricultural inputs.

Figure 4 summarises the three broad 'streams' in the value chain where the policies and practices of a FMCG company such as UI may have significant impacts on workers, consumers, communities, and the environment. The three streams are *quality control* (incorporating consumer safety); *environmental responsibility* (incorporating, for example, resource use, pollution, transport, and packaging); and *social responsibility* (incorporating, for example, safety, working conditions, and pay). From UI's perspective, the need to ensure quality and safety for consumers has driven a careful analysis and management of the backward and forward linkages for each product. These quality drivers have increasingly tended to include environmental and social issues.

Figure 4: UI and its business partners: from sourcing to marketplace

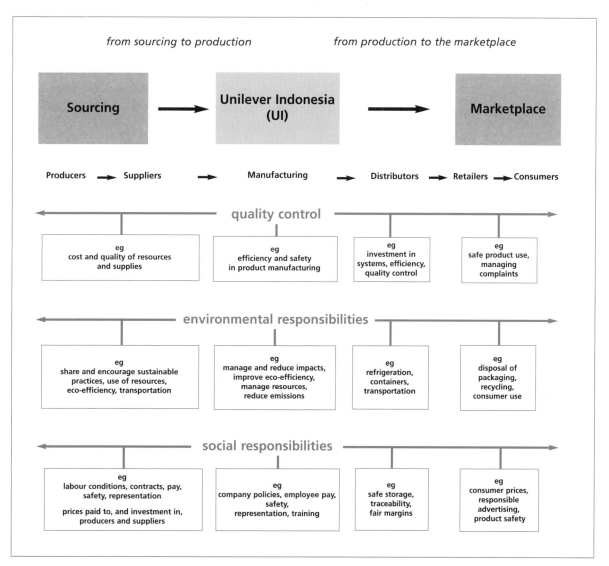

Adapted with permission from models developed by The Corporate Citizenship Company

Supplier companies

The purchasing policies and practices of large companies can have a range of positive and negative impacts on supplier companies, and, in turn, on people working in the supply chain. A purchasing company negotiating a major supply contract may make a range of stipulations relating to the quality and standards required of the product, the delivery date and price of the final product, and the length of the contract. These factors may have a negative impact on workers' wages and conditions. On the other hand, contracts may attempt to ensure that the conditions required for achieving goals relating to quality and working standards will be put in place. Such contracts may secure better terms and working conditions for workers. Decisions about where and what to purchase, and from whom, and how often to change suppliers, have onward impacts on the livelihood security of workers within the supply chain.

UI purchases a wide range of goods and services from its supplier companies. While some raw materials and manufactured goods are bought abroad and imported for manufacturing in Indonesia, UI purchases the great majority of its goods and services (84 per cent – see below) through a local supply chain, made up of Indonesian and international companies with operations in Indonesia. The supply chain behind these purchases represents a major economic multiplier effect of UI's local investment, with wide potential impacts on the livelihoods of people living in poverty in Indonesia.

An overview of UI's relationships with supplier companies in Indonesia

The majority of UI's business is in the home and personal-care sector. Many, but not all, ingredients used to make the personal-care and household products that UI sells are either chemical-based or made from highly refined agricultural materials. Chemicals are the largest single set of UI purchases, representing 9 per cent of all purchases.[20]

In 2003, UI worked with 334 suppliers, spending approximately Rp 3,591 billion (US$ 419 million). Of these, 265 suppliers were domestic, and 69 were international companies. Domestic suppliers provided 84 per cent of goods and services, while overseas suppliers provided 16 per cent of the total. Some supplier companies were set up with support from UI to supply it with key goods and services to the quality standards that it requires. Today, UI represents on average only 15–25 per cent of the sales of these suppliers.

In 2003, the top ten suppliers (by value) were all Indonesian companies, accounting for 34 per cent of all UI purchases in that year. The average duration of these suppliers' working relationship with UI is 15 years. Some 90 per cent of all suppliers and contract purchasers / co-packers (CPs) have written contracts. The arrangements not covered by written contracts relate to occasional or irregular purchases.[21] Some 30 per cent of suppliers are audited for product quality each year. Research for this report suggests that UI does not break contracts with its suppliers, and that contracts generally run from six months to a year before they are renewed. This emphasis on building long-term relationships with supplier companies is likely to reduce job insecurity within the supply chain.

Perhaps the single most important impact of UI's overall business strategy is that it creates opportunities for local entrepreneurs to supply UI's various needs. In fact, the company operates many programmes that are designed to identify, work with, and foster the growth of local entrepreneurs and SMEs, as local sourcing is clearly a benefit to UI. Most of this influence is possible because UI has limited its focus to manufacturing and marketing, so it is not competing with potential partners. This gives opportunities to a wide range of individuals and companies in Indonesia to become directly involved in the UI supply or distribution chain.

In general, after three–four years of close support, UI begins to encourage more independence in the suppliers' business strategy and management. UI continues to serve as an intermediary with banks and to advise suppliers about borrowing and loan-repayment strategies to help their credit rating.

Terms and conditions for workers in the supplier companies of UI

All 334 suppliers are required by UI to sign its Code of Business Principles, which seeks to promote a range of ethical, social, and environmental standards. Through negotiations and on-going dialogue, UI encourages supplier companies to maintain ethical standards and other standards over and above its requirement for suppliers to adhere to all national laws. For example, Indonesian law requires that children are not employed, and that employers pay a minimum wage. In addition, UI encourages suppliers to pay at least 10 per cent above the legal minimum wage. (The norm in Indonesia tends to be lower than the official minimum wage. It is standard practice for many small firms to count transportation costs and meal allowances toward the 'minimum wage', in effect paying a base salary of only 75 per cent of the government's official minimum wage.)

UI says that, in practice, its suppliers and other partners pay even higher wages than this and offer better packages, including benefits such as meal, medical, and annual allowances (for the observance of festivals and Ramadan). UI estimates that the average wage payments made by its partners are 158 per cent of what is required by law in Indonesia (see Table 8). Nevertheless, the research team's interviews with a small number of employees and workers in supplier companies and within UI indicated that pay and conditions among supplier companies are generally less generous than within UI.

Table 8: UI estimates of average monthly payments to entry-level workers (Java) paid by UI third-party partners (2003)

Expense	UI partner payment (Rp)	UI partner payment ($)	Indonesian minimum wage (Rp)	Indonesian minimum wage ($)
Minimum salary	694,100	81	631,554	73.7
Annual allowance	86,763	10.1	0	0
Insurance allowance	31,235	3.65	0	0
Meal allowance	187,500	21.9	0	0

Source: UI

As with UI, it is probable that a good number of suppliers employ contract workers. UI does not keep records or require its suppliers to submit records of their use of contract workers. The research found in two companies surveyed that contract workers made up 15 per cent and 40 per cent respectively of the supplier workforce.

Over time, UI's business strategy has come to focus on high-volume, high-technology, and high value-added operations. It has outsourced parts of the operation that were self-contained and non-proprietary, ranging from professional services to some of the more labour-intensive aspects of production. In this way UI has reduced capital, management, and oversight costs, while at the same time building production capacity elsewhere among independent companies within Indonesia. UI works in partnership with and invests in many third-party manufacturers, for example by providing raw materials, packaging, machinery, and other equipment, as well as technical assistance.

In addition to encouraging adherence to Unilever's Code of Business Principles, UI requires every supplier's overall policies and practices to be monitored as part of the annual evaluation for the Preferred Supplier Programme. Over three years, all suppliers are audited. UI suppliers are required to meet the same global standards for environment, health and safety as it does itself. As a consequence, UI has had to invest in overhauling the production systems within its SME partners to comply with requirements for quality, quantity, timeliness of deliveries, and protection of both occupational health and safety in the workplace and the natural environment. UI has developed training strategies with technical assistance and close supervisory support for each partner. In addition, it has developed systems to penalise those partners that do not meet its standards. UI reports that the ultimate penalty of contract termination has been enforced only once in the history of its partnerships.

UI emphasises that the key to its successful partnerships with suppliers is that it does not have adversarial relationships with its partners. UI reports that there have been no legal actions either by or against its suppliers during the past ten years. UI works with its partners over time to achieve and maintain standards. For all parties, this is an on-going learning experience, based on mutual self-interest. UI tries to improve performance, rather than relying on enforcing compliance, and looks for common ground to reduce negative impacts and maintain standards. This approach extends to cost management. Oxfam believes that expanding these requirements to apply to labour standards would increase UI's positive influence on labour rights in the supply chain.

UI buys large volumes of goods and services, and negotiates volume discounts with suppliers. According to the research, UI is the largest and most valued client for most of its suppliers. In the course of the research, some suppliers explained that low prices, due either to high volume reductions negotiated by UI or simply a drop in the market price, have sometimes forced them to require lower prices back through their own supply chain, in order to meet UI's requirements. This can have adverse effects on farmers and other raw-material suppliers (as well as those who work for them), who have the least bargaining power in the value chain.

Some inputs, like crude palm oil and coconut oil (used for soap manufacture) have traditionally been available in Indonesia. Box 5 illustrates UI's policy of encouraging the sourcing of products and ingredients from within Indonesia.

Box 5: Examples of UI sourcing in Indonesia

Toothpaste

Local calcium carbonate has replaced imported ingredients (e.g. dicalcium phosphate) as the abrasive agent in toothpaste (this is 45 per cent of product formulation). Sorbitol (some 27 per cent of toothpaste formulation) is now produced from cassava grown by 15,000 local farmers, rather than imported. Case Study 1 (page 66) discusses how the supplier PT Sorini affects local production of cassava. UI's flavouring supplier is attempting to grow peppermint in Indonesia (imported peppermint is currently the single most costly input for toothpaste).

Packaging materials

In the past, packaging and packing materials were imported. Now they are produced locally. They include those made from wood fibres and paper, as well as high-technology plastics like flexi-packaging and laminate web. Case Study 2 (page 67) reports on how Dai Nippon, a packaging supplier, is influenced by UI.

Shampoo

Detergent surfactants are produced in Indonesia by Cognis Indonesia and PT Indokemindo (in Surabaya). Case Study 3 (page 79) discusses how the manufacture of shampoo, which consists of highly processed inputs rather than agricultural inputs, can have an impact on the lives of poor people.

Yet the opportunities that a globalised economy creates for MNCs like Unilever pose dilemmas and trade-offs that can affect this positive policy of local sourcing. For example, in the future it may be better to manufacture a product such as toothpaste in one Asian regional centre rather than in several countries, either because of cost savings, or because a plant elsewhere is more efficient and/or run to high environmental standards. The benefits of this would have to be weighed against the higher transportation costs, local regulations, cultural preferences, and risks posed by a single source of supply. Oxfam would ask that the relevant stakeholders, such as workers or local communities likely to be affected, were consulted about such decisions as transparently and sensitively as possible.

Case study 1: Economic and employment impacts in the UI supply chain: the case of PT Sorini, a supplier of raw materials[22]

PT Sorini, a company based in East Java, was founded in 1983 to supply UI with sorbitol, a major ingredient of toothpaste. Sorbitol is made from starch extracted from cassava, which is purchased from farmers in East Java. By 2003, Sorini purchased some 80,000 MT of cassava per annum. Optimum cassava yields are 8 MT/hectare, and the growing time is roughly eight months. Since each farmer owns 0.25 ha on average, it is estimated that this market is supplied directly by some 200,000 farmers. Sorini now exports 70 per cent of its production to 55 countries. UI buys approximately 20 per cent of the company's total production.

PT Sorini has 400 employees, and most of them come from the local area. Two per cent of employees are women. According to UI's assessment, PT Sorini pays entry-level workers about 10 per cent more than the regional legal minimum wage. Other benefits (such as health-care allowances, leave of absence, overtime pay, and maternity leave) comply with or exceed government regulations. The company also provides on-going training for workers.

PT Sorini uses water from the local area in its processing plant. In 2003 the company made a voluntary donation of Rp 25 million to the village for the use of water in processing and manufacturing sorbitol, thus providing an additional incentive for the village to keep the water clean.[23] PT Sorini also supports domestic waste, public health, and community-development programmes in the local village. Sorini works with local raw-material producers to find useful ways to dispose of the company's solid and liquid waste: by using it for feeding cattle and watering crops, respectively.

In support of PT Sorini and other suppliers, UI is helping to find ways of working more directly with primary producers to ensure product quality and quantity. This benefits UI, because it ensures a steady supply of inputs of consistent quality; it also benefits the producers, because it is a dependable market for high-volume sales and reduced transaction costs. Such win–win solutions can benefit both buyer and seller, without necessarily making either unduly dependent on the other.

Case study 2: Economic and employment impacts in the UI supply chain: the case of Dai Nippon, a packaging supplier[24]

Dai Nippon is a printing and product-packing company with 2,500 employees. Founded in 1972, it was dedicated to supplying UI. Over time this has changed: while UI is still Dai Nippon's largest single client (25 per cent of sales), the company also works with a wide range of other clients.

UI has had a large impact on Dai Nippon. Their relationship shows that multinational companies can encourage good business practices, as well as corporate social responsibility, among smaller national companies. UI helped the company to address management problems and has provided technical assistance on a range of issues facing the company. Today, Dai Nippon is broadly respected in its own right and competes in both domestic and international markets.

According to UI's assessment, in addition to overall management and product-quality issues, UI has influenced Dai Nippon's employment and environmental policies and practices. For example, the company has two medical centres for employees, staffed by doctors and nurses. Every employee is required to have a free medical check-up each year. The company also provides child care for its employees.

Each year, UI undertakes a supplier-quality assessment. Dai Nippon has been awarded the status of Preferred Supplier (evaluated according to its management, quality, logistics and delivery, technical services, prices, plant safety, and environmental impacts) for the past four years.

Producers of raw materials

Some of the products that UI sells are made from a range of Indonesian raw materials, which are sourced from a large number of diverse producers, traders, and processors. The five major agricultural raw materials entering UI's local supply chain are tea, palm oil, cassava, black soybean, and coconut sugar. Many of the producers[25] growing these crops are among the poorest people in UI's value chain. As a result, the potential impact of pro-poor supply-chain policies directed at primary producers is considerable.

In assessing impacts on the poor, it is important to note that most of UI's purchases of these raw agricultural materials are made from traders and processors, not from poor agricultural producers directly. The 'primary producers' of these materials are usually several transactions removed from UI. While a large company's purchasing policies and practices can have major impacts on employment, working conditions, and basic wages for those who work for its suppliers and their suppliers in turn, it is clear that these positive impacts tend to be weakened as they move farther out along the value chain. How should the relative advantages and disadvantages of operating in the supply chains of major companies be weighed, as against selling into traditional markets?

Oxfam describes 'alternative supply chains' as those that increase the market power, income, savings and/or choice of poor producers in their interaction with companies. This can be accomplished through direct purchasing at higher prices, by pre-financing production, or by direct bargaining on prices between producers or producer associations and buyers, for example.

The detailed case study in the next section sets out UI's progress in partnering with black-soy producers to develop an alternative to the traditional supply chain.

Kecap Bango sweet soy sauce: from farm to fork

It was beyond the scope of this project to analyse all of UI's relationships with primary producers. Instead, this section examines the case of one product in detail: Kecap Bango sweet soy sauce, made from two agricultural products that are sourced locally. This research explored whether, under UI management, the product provides a reasonable share of benefits to its suppliers, especially the poor farmers producing the raw materials.

Kecap Bango is one of several types of sweet soy sauce produced in Indonesia. Although the brand is based in Java, it was poised for national distribution when it was purchased by UI in 2001, selected because of its existing market, the strengths of the company, and the expected appeal of the product formulation for national distribution. Under UI's management, the sales of Kecap Bango underwent rapid growth. Due to UI's marketing, sales of the product have increased 425 per cent: from 4,000 MT per year in 2000 to 21,000 MT in 2003. By 2003, the total margins generated by Kecap Bango from sale of raw-material inputs, as well as the value generated through processing, manufacturing, branding, and retail sales, are estimated at Rp 58 billion. UI's gross margin on the manufacture and sale of the product is Rp 20.4 billion, or 35.8 per cent of the estimated value of the product as it moves through the value chain.[26]

Kecap Bango represents just 1.8 per cent of UI's sales, but its supply chain was chosen for study because it represents a novel way in which UI has responded locally to the need for expansion of an agriculturally based product.

Box 6: Palm oil and tea

At the global level, Unilever is a major buyer and exporter from Indonesia of both palm oil and tea. During the period July 2003–June 2004, Unilever bought approximately 570,000 MT of palm oil in Indonesia, of which the local Unilever Indonesian business used about 85,000 MT, or 14 per cent of the total. These purchases represent 5.1 and 0.7 per cent of Indonesian production, and 1.8 and 0.25 of global production. Similarly, Unilever is a major buyer of tea from Indonesia: more than 30,000 MT, which represents approximately one per cent of annual global production, 2 per cent of global exports, and 25 per cent of Indonesia's tea exports.[27]

Unilever is participating in the Roundtable on Sustainable Palm Oil, which is developing standards for plantation establishment, as well as better practices to reduce the industry's negative social and environmental impacts. Similarly, Unilever has developed extensive guidelines on better management practices (BMPs) for tea production, and it participates in the Ethical Tea Partnership.

In 2002, UI initiated a pilot project to source one of its ingredients directly from farmers. Because sales had increased dramatically since UI acquired the brand, the company needed to find ways to secure a constantly expanding supply of black soybeans of consistent quality, suitable for making Kecap Bango. (Gearing up production in the near term to match market demand was made more difficult because it takes nine months to ferment the black soybeans.) These opportunities and bottlenecks gave impetus to UI's work with primary producers to secure sources to satisfy future demand. In addition, black soy is a new and relatively minor agricultural raw material for UI, a fact which made it easier for the company to intervene in the value chain.

The ingredients of Kecap Bango are agricultural products that have been produced in Indonesia for a very long time: coconut sugar, soy sauce made from fermented black soybeans, and brine. Black soy has been produced for centuries in Indonesia and is commonly used to make sweet soy sauce. Coconut sugar represents more than 80 per cent of the product by weight, and a high proportion of the volume as an input. Both of these products are labour-intensive and traditionally are produced by and sourced from a labyrinth of small farmers and traders. Neither of these products is grown on plantations.

The number of coconut-sugar producers and black-soy farmers supplying the current level of production of Kecap Bango is estimated at 13,815 (see Figure 5). Thus, while Kecap Bango represents a very small proportion of UI's total sales, the people producing and trading in the Kecap Bango supply chain are a much larger proportion of the estimated employment within UI's entire supply chain. It is one of UI's more labour-intensive products.

Considerable research from around the world has found that small-scale agricultural producers are usually the least advantaged participants in a value chain. For this product, the black-soybean producers have more advantages than the coconut-sugar producers, because they hold more negotiating power in transactions with traders and companies. First, the demand for black soybean is strong, because it is a 'niche' product and there is a limited number of producers, whereas there is a large supply of coconut sugar, compared with demand. Second, because coconut-sugar producers are usually dependent on credit from the traders who buy their production, they are in a weak bargaining position when selling their commodity.

Black-soybean production is highly specialised. Locally, there is little quality control or consistency of product: there are some 46 varieties of black soybean in production, which are often mixed in the marketplace. With increasing demand for high-quality black soybeans throughout Java, UI was concerned to maintain sufficient supply. When UI first acquired Kecap Bango, all purchases were made through traders. However, the company moved to develop a pilot programme to create an alternative supply chain for the crop, sourcing more directly from producers to improve overall quality, stimulate production, ensure sufficient supplies as markets expanded, and, if possible, reduce costs.

Figure 5: Coconut-sugar and black-soybean producers, collectors, and traders involved in the Kecap Bango supply chain (2000–2003)

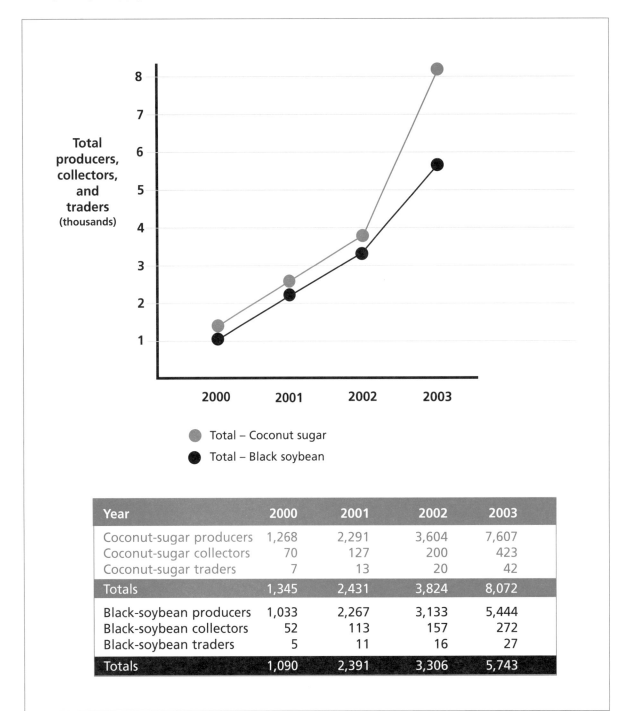

Year	2000	2001	2002	2003
Coconut-sugar producers	1,268	2,291	3,604	7,607
Coconut-sugar collectors	70	127	200	423
Coconut-sugar traders	7	13	20	42
Totals	1,345	2,431	3,824	8,072
Black-soybean producers	1,033	2,267	3,133	5,444
Black-soybean collectors	52	113	157	272
Black-soybean traders	5	11	16	27
Totals	1,090	2,391	3,306	5,743

While many local farmers were interested in producing black soybeans to sell to UI, even those with experience of planting local black-soybean varieties had to learn about the new variety developed by Gajah Mada University in Yogyakarta. The university and UI worked together to develop and improve the quality of new soybean seeds, develop certified seed sources, identify more reliable production methods, provide credit, and guarantee farmers purchase of the product at a contracted price. UI developed a similar partnership with Rabo Bank in the area of Nganjuk and Trenggalek (East Java) to identify the best systems to produce and sell black soybeans. UI also supported the development of mechanical threshing and improved storage systems to retain product quality and reduce post-harvest losses.

In 2002 Gajah Mada University started working with about a dozen farmers. In 2003 they worked with nearly 400 farmers, most of whom had planted yellow or traditional black soybeans in the past. These farmers plant three crops per year—two of rice and usually one of peanuts or another cash crop. Income from their third crop represents about one-third of their farming income, and in turn less than half of their overall household income.

Of the 1,000 MT of black soybeans that UI purchased in 2002, 90 per cent came through traditional market traders, while the alternative trading system with its pilot farms accounted for about 100 MT. However, the number of farmers selling through the alternative value chain is expanding rapidly. In the last two years the programme has expanded at a rate of 50–75 per cent per year, with more than 1,000 farmers participating at the beginning of 2004. This expansion appears to be set to continue.

UI is gaining security of supply, and consistent quality of a product that is essential for one of its fastest-growing specialist brands. Farmers' interest in participating is evidenced by the growing number of applications. But why are farmers eager to join the programme, and why is UI eager to expand it? Three benefits are security of markets, the availability of credit from UI, and the university's technical assistance, financed by UI. In addition, direct purchases by UI gave farmers a 10–15 per cent higher price than that on offer from traditional traders. In the traditional purchasing arrangements of UI, soy producers receive only a proportion of the price that UI pays to traders for their products. The alternative trading system reduces the dominance of middlemen, so soy producers can receive a greater share of the UI price. Crucially for poor and small-scale farmers, the up-front investment represents an opportunity to access credit, guaranteed markets, and technical assistance that they would not otherwise be able to afford.

Several outstanding issues remain. Not all farmers have made such gains. There have been some crop failures. In some cases the quality of part of the product was substandard and rejected by company buyers. For most farmers the yields have been less than those achieved by the demonstration plots at the university.

In 2003, about 20 per cent of the first crop was rejected on the grounds of poor quality. UI asked the farmers to re-sort the soybeans for quality, and the rejects were sold at lower prices to the local market. Because some of those farmers made a loss rather than a profit, they were unable to repay the loans to UI. UI extended the deadline for repayment (without interest) to the following harvest season, but farmers still bear liability for the credit. Such issues are not normally in evidence except far down the supply chain, and they are not usually seen or addressed by a large company buying raw materials from traders.

To ensure market access for small producers, some form of organising is required. In this example, a more direct relationship with UI has increased some farmers' incomes, at least in the short term, and has encouraged them to diversify their planting beyond rice and peanuts. Depending on the observer's perspective, black soy can be seen as increasing farmers' reliance upon a cash crop, or increasing by one the number of crops that they are able to sell. Black-soybean production does not, however, appear to reduce in any way the farmers' production of rice, their main food crop, since two rice crops are still planted on the farms where black soybeans are grown. The crop does, however, increase farmers' dependence on a single buyer. But contracts for black soybeans lock in prices at the time of planting rather than at the time of harvest, when prices usually are more depressed. This form of contract farming is becoming more common around the world, because companies want to increase product quality and guarantee supply. The system creates opportunities for both the company and the producers, but some elements of risk remain.

Oxfam is concerned that UI's pilot work on soybeans might undermine traditional credit and market relationships on which farmers depend for other crops. While these systems are exploitative at many levels, they also provide farmers with capital needed for non-farm expenses, for example medical needs, school fees, and the costs of weddings and funerals. The new credit system provided through UI is cheaper, more efficient, and interest-free to farmers, but it can be used only for expenses related to producing black soybeans. Oxfam considers that farmers risk becoming over-dependent upon UI for the sale of the crop, and that they would be hurt by any decline in demand. While producers may benefit from this new system, there are producers and traders in the old supply chain who lose out by exclusion from the new supply chain.

From UI's point of view, direct purchasing of black soy has higher overall transaction costs for the company. It is far more complicated and, as a consequence, in some ways riskier than buying directly from traders. Some of UI's cost can be seen as an up-front investment whose costs can be amortised by increasing purchases from a larger group of producers.

UI is currently analysing how this sourcing system fits with its overall business strategy. Buying black soybeans directly from farmers is an experiment for UI, and the quantity purchased is still only a small proportion of its total black-soybean purchases. While currently UI has no plan to buy all of its black-soybean requirements more directly from local farmers, such a move would extend the opportunities to more poor households. However, it would not be simple to extend the alternative trading system for black soybeans, or to apply the model to other crop-supply chains.

Coconut-sugar producers

Our research also investigated the production of coconut sugar. UI has not, to date, undertaken an alternative-trading pilot scheme with coconut-sugar farmers, because of the complexity of the chain and the ready availability of an expanding supply.

As observed above, coconut-sugar producers lack the bargaining power of farmers who sell a 'niche' product like black soybeans which is in great demand. Sugar producers' bargaining position with the traders to whom they sell their commodity is further weakened by the fact that they are often in debt to them.

Coconut sugar goes through a long supply chain before it reaches UI, and there are three types of such chain, of varying degrees of complexity. Margins are added at each layer, set by those traders who directly supply the ingredients to companies like UI. UI purchased 3,550 tons of coconut sugar in 2000, a figure which had increased to 21,300 tons by 2003. In that year UI purchased coconut sugar from seven supplier companies. The research found no significant difference between the price paid for coconut sugar purchased by UI for Kecap Bango and that paid by other companies. In other words, without an intentional supply-chain intervention, it would be unusual for companies to pay more than the market price. UI is looking into the possibility of creating an alternative supply chain for coconut sugar, but has not so far been able to identify a viable model.

Coconut sugar is produced year-round by households dedicated to its production. It could represent the total production effort of more than 6,000 households. Those households who tap the coconut palm are the least advantaged participants in the sweet soy sauce value chain. Most small-scale producers are locked into a constant cycle of dependency. The needs of daily consumption drive them to borrow money from village buyers, offering their crops as collateral. In turn, this debt forces them to sell their crops to the same collectors. If labour costs are included, using the local minimum wage as a guide, these producers actually experience negative profit margins – but this does not make them switch to other products, because they have no other choices.

Yet there are opportunities for producers themselves, and those interested in supporting them, to improve their position in the value chain. Micro and small-scale producers who are well organised are able to sell more directly to the open market, thereby receiving a better price for their product. They can do this by pooling their production, for example, or by finding transportation to enable them to deliver directly to traders.

The potential poverty impacts of buying coconut sugar more directly are even more striking than for black soy, for the following reasons: producers are poorer; UI purchases much more coconut sugar than black soy; and coconut-sugar production is more labour-intensive than soy. If UI was able to create an alternative coconut-sugar supply chain, it could potentially benefit producers through improved prices, guaranteed markets, and reduced debt, while providing itself with a more reliable supply of a higher-quality product, at the same or even a lower price. But while discussions continue about creating alternative supply chains for coconut sugar, at present UI's alternative arrangements with black-soy producers are the only such pilot.

In the case of Kecap Bango, the number of people affected by the production and sale of the product is far greater on the supply side than on the distribution side. This is due to the labour-intensive nature of the raw-material inputs, as well as the fact that the product has only recently been marketed nationally. While production is likely to remain labour-intensive, increased sales would increase employment generated through distribution as well.

The distribution chain

The sections above have described impacts on poverty in UI's supply chain. This section shifts the focus to analysis of the distribution and retail end of the UI value chain. Many studies of the impacts of the activities of large companies on poor people have focused on the experiences of poor producers and workers in the supply chain and in company operations. But because UI markets the majority of its products within Indonesia, the forward linkages to distributors and retailers in its value chain also have significant impacts.

UI's distribution and retail chain is complex, integrating several different types of actor. UI distributes its products through two retail channels: large, medium, and small general trade/grocery stores across the country (referred to as *general trade* and accounting for about 80 per cent of sales) and self-service stores and supermarkets (the latter being referred to as *modern trade*, and accounting for about 20 per cent of sales). Modern trade focuses on big accounts such as Carrefour, Hero, and Indomaret. UI distributes its products directly to modern-trade outlets. General trade is co-ordinated through 385 distributor firms and 1,267 SDKs (Sub-Distributor Kecamatan), which are independent businesses. UI supplies its product to major distributors at the same price throughout the country, regardless of the transport costs. In turn, through its distributors and sub-distributors it advises retailers to sell UI products at a recommended retail price (RRP).

In general, distributors earn margins of 4.5 per cent, while SDK-system distributors and sub-distributors earn margins of 1.5 per cent and 3 per cent respectively. In a deflationary market where unit sales prices are falling, growing sales volume is needed if UI and its distributors and retailers are to maintain and enhance their earnings.

Once products are beyond the control of UI's distributors, final sale prices to end-consumers, and the margins that retailers earn, vary considerably. Non-UI distributors and retailers may choose not to sell UI's products at the manufacturer's recommended retail price. Additional mark-ups tend to be lower in competitive urban markets and higher in more isolated, rural areas. Thus, as in many other countries, consumers in rural areas tend to pay more for the same products than people who live in urban areas.

Some recent trends in the support provided by UI to the different distribution systems of both the general and the modern trade are noteworthy.

- **General trade:** the SDK system of micro-distribution was deliberately created by UI to reach consumers whom it could not reach on its own. This has resulted in 1,267 mostly blue-collar workers becoming business partners, with permitted margins and a bonus incentive for total sales. Ice-cream hawkers using bicycle-powered carts, and sidewalk stall owners selling ready-to-eat noodles serve main streets and small alleys in the city. Thousands of them are engaged in distributing UI's products.

- **Modern trade:** according to UI, teams of female promotions staff in modern-trade and grocery-store outlets have been upgraded to 'Sales Push Teams' (still mostly women), and, as a consequence, their status and earnings have improved. This group represents a new sales force for UI, using new marketing techniques such as consumer advice to promote Unilever brands. They also relay to UI important information on consumer trends and concerns. In return they receive salaries, social insurance, allowances, bonuses, and regular training. UI has engaged two small/medium enterprise (SME) training agents to manage this programme.

Box 7: Distribution and livelihoods

In Indonesia, UI has worked with its distributors to develop a network of well-motivated sub-distributors that covers an ever-increasing area of the country. In a highly competitive marketplace, effective distribution of products to consumers is essential.

To establish this network, UI deliberately works in partnership with a wide range of independent distributors, and through them with an even larger number of sub-distributors. For example, at the sub-distribution level, UI believes that it has worked with almost 1,267 individuals,

helping them to become business owners and entrepreneurs. They require at least a secondary-school education, and previously most were semi-skilled workers, many of whom lost their employment in businesses as a result of the economic crisis. Today, each of these individuals runs a business with an average of one additional employee, often a member of the family. They make a 3 per cent margin on a turnover that ranges from about Rp 11,700,000 to Rp 442,000,000. They receive bonuses for outstanding sales. The distributor provides

to the sub-distributors one month's worth of goods (valued at Rp 6 million, or US$ 706) as working capital. This assistance helps to solve the credit problems that would confront most of these individuals if they had to borrow money from more formal financial institutions. UI also provides training in merchandising, selling, and marketing, as well as stock control and book-keeping. Such businesses can be 'stepping stones', providing skills and experience to new entrepreneurs entering the formal economy.

General trade is co-ordinated through 385 distributors and 1,267 SDKs. UI estimates that its general-trade distribution system supplies its brands directly to 550,000 small retailers. These include small stores; small family-run shops, often inside a family's dwelling, called *warungs*; and small retail stalls in urban and rural areas. Company officials believe that an estimated 1.8 million similar small outlets also carry UI products, which they buy directly from independent distributors or supermarkets.[28]

Unlike its suppliers, many UI distributors tend to be smaller (averaging only 25–60 employees) and more directly linked, dependent partners of UI. Also unlike suppliers, of the five distributors interviewed as part of this research, some complained that it is more expensive to work with UI than with other FMCG companies, because they are required to maintain computerised inventories which impose costs that reduce distributor profits. Little bargaining is allowed, because the prices and margins are set in advance. UI requires such systems, however, because they improve inventory management and provide traceability of product, which is important for consumer safety, so there are no plans to change the system.

Of the distributors interviewed, some complained that they receive products that they had not ordered because UI added some, through UI's 'allocation' system. Distributors maintain that there are excess stocks at UI's warehouse, often products with low sales value, that are distributed without prior notice. This can cause distributors to have difficulties in cash-flow management if they cannot return the products. Similar complaints were made in respect of products that are damaged in shipping, or when there is disruption in supply, either between distributors, or because UI is supplying products to large stores.

UI has policies to avoid such problems. The 'allocation' system was originally designed for new products in cases where advance notice cannot be given, for competition and confidentiality reasons. And a system for compensating distributors for damaged stock has been worked out and reduced to a standard percentage allowance for administrative convenience. The research has identified some gaps in applying UI policies: findings that could be helpful in further improving the business partnership between general-trade distributors and UI.

The UI distribution system promotes entrepreneurship, employment, and profitability in SMEs throughout the distribution chain. Indonesia's retail sector underwent a fundamental restructuring after the 1997 financial crisis, so most small retailers and distributors started (or re-started) their businesses after the crisis. Today, UI's 385 distributors employ more than three times the number of people employed by UI directly.

Not surprisingly, the research team found that employment conditions within distributing companies are not as good as among UI's direct workforce or among supplier companies. This is probably because of their much smaller size, and the lower skill level required of their employees, compared with people working in supplier companies. Although the sample size of eight distributor firms was small, the results were similar across those interviewed. For example, the employees did not feel very secure in their jobs (a state of affairs that was in marked contrast with job-tenure rates at UI); none of the respondents had knowledge of a Collective Labour Agreement that applied to them; and the majority reported that they did not have contracts with their companies. Furthermore, they commented that they had not received pay for overtime work done, because of the nature of the work. On the positive side, most said that they had the right to make suggestions on their wage levels; the two contract workers among them received pay while on leave; there were no reported accidents; and most of them received training that they appreciated. Given how valuable this employment opportunity is for such individuals, it would be worth exploring how employment conditions could be strengthened in this part of the value chain in a way that is feasible in business terms.

The project research suggests that UI's products could represent some 10 per cent of the sales value of all product sales in small local shops and *warungs.* This means that of the conservatively estimated 1,653,000 jobs and livelihoods involved at the point of sale in these shops (see Box 8 on page 80), the equivalent of 165,300 (ten per cent of the total) could be supported by the sale of UI products. Assuming that all small stores earn approximately the same income, then Rp 33,750 from each of 550,000 small stores can be attributed to UI's products. The total value from sales of UI products in small stores is estimated at Rp 18.6 billion, or US$ 2.2 million.

Retail sales by sub-distributors are embedded in a web of other income-generation activities. For example, four *warungs* in Bekasi, Java, make an average monthly profit of Rp 337,500 (not quite US$ 40/month), or some 42 per cent of total family income. Many family members earn income by working as labourers, or they have other additional employment. And in many cases, poor families themselves consume some of the goods on sale in their *warungs,* or they support other poor households. So while *warung* activity brings income and assets to households, it is difficult to judge from this research the extent of income generation and savings associated with the small retailers farthest along the chain. Whether and how UI or other large companies can improve economic development for small-scale retailers is an area for further study.

Warung owners interviewed for this research say that they sell a variety of FMCG products and brands, including some UI brands. Consumer preference and product quality are the main reason why they sell UI products. The margins on UI products are less than those of competitors' products, because they tend to have higher wholesale prices, and local retailers feel that they can mark them up only so much before people will stop buying them. Still, owners say that branded products such as those sold by UI and other FMGC companies are what bring people to the stores. In short, in addition to selling UI products, they benefit from simply having them on the shelves.

Finally, UI is also encouraging the development of street sales of various food products. For example, UI's policy of selling ice cream through 21,000 street vendors, who walk or use bicycles to sell the product, engages those vendors in entry-level commerce. Similarly, UI's support for sidewalk food vendors also has the potential to increase not only business skills – including health and safety practices – but income and employment as well. Such approaches can work in favour of poor people when a company targets and helps to train poor people to become vendors, as UI programmes currently do.

Supporting employment and value generation in UI's value chain

This final section presents an overview of the employment and cash value generated by and distributed to the various participants in UI's value chain. Although this overview cannot give direct information about the poverty impacts of the value chain, it offers important data showing the relative spread of employment and value generated by a company like UI that is deeply embedded in the economy.

Employment

UI has 3,096 permanent employees, including 184 temporary employees. It has another 1,989 contract workers. An additional 1,800 people are employed by co-packers and third-party producers in the UI value chain. On the supply side of the value chain, it is estimated that some 105,000 people are employed on a full-time equivalent basis (see Box 8 on page 80) as suppliers or producers of raw materials that are used to manufacture UI products. This includes producers of soybeans, sugar, palm oil, tea, cassava, and the many other raw materials that go into UI's products. On the distribution side, it is estimated that around 188,000 full-time equivalent jobs and other forms of livelihood are supported through the sale of UI products.

Even with incomplete information, it is possible to estimate credibly that UI's economic activities support in varying degrees some 300,000 jobs and livelihoods in Indonesia. More than half of this impact is in its distribution system, especially in UI-supplied *warungs*, and about one third in its supply chain. Figure 6 on page 82 summarises the total employment data linked to UI's value chain.

On the supply side, there is the known or estimated employment in supplier companies, and – as is illustrated in the Kecap Bango study – in raw-material suppliers and traders.

Home-care and personal-care products are manufactured with ingredients that come mainly from highly processed inputs and industrial processes. While these products have limited impact on employment generation on the supply side, they do result in considerable employment on the distribution and retail side, which has implications for reducing poverty. See Case Study 3.

Case Study 3: Shampoo – from creation to consumption

Unlike UI food products such as Kecap Bango, shampoo products are manufactured with ingredients that come mainly from highly processed inputs such as chemicals, and water. As a consequence, the employment impacts on the supply side are limited, particularly compared with products made from agricultural ingredients where more people are involved in the supply chain. Thus for shampoo the employment impacts are far greater on the distribution and retail sides, where more people will be employed, both directly and indirectly. This has implications for reducing poverty, and implies that expanding total product sales could become, at least for essential products, a policy for employment.

For example, in 2003, sachets of UI's best-selling shampoo brand had become the most popular package size, representing 7.3 per cent of the company's total sales. From this it can be calculated that sales of these shampoo sachets are linked to some 13,700 FTE jobs in UI's distribution system alone. UI's margin on the sales of its best-selling shampoo was about one third of the total margins generated (see Table 9 below). In short, others received in total twice the margin that UI received from the sales of shampoo through the value chain.

Table 9: Estimate of gross margins generated by UI's best-selling shampoo in the value chain (2003)[29]

	Total product sales (Rp millions)	Gross margin (% of sales)	Gross margin by value (Rp millions)
Producer	Rp 482,303.2	10	Rp 48,230.3
Processor	Rp 513,088.5	6	Rp 30,785.3
UI	Rp 596,614.5	14	Rp 83,526.0
Distributor	Rp 620,479.1	4.5	Rp 27,921.6
Retailer	Rp 688,731.8	11	Rp 68,252.7

UI itself generates permanent employment, as well as temporary and contract employment, through its own dedicated manufacturing plants. In UI's distribution system, many are earning an income by selling UI products. The jobs cover the broad spectrum of Indonesian society. They introduce a large number of individuals, for the first time, to a relatively predictable income flow. They can be seen as exemplifying the first steps in the development of a formal modern economy. Figure 6 on page 82 summarises the employment data linked to UI's value chain.[30]

Box 8: Calculating employment supported in the value chain

In this chapter, the term 'full-time equivalent' (FTE) is used in estimates of employment supported in the UI value chain. FTE calculations can be easily misunderstood. An FTE is an artificial construct, intended to give a sense of the total amount of full-time employment supported by an organisation's economic activity. FTEs are a way to convert part-time jobs or sources of income (such as those of workers, farmers, or retailers with multiple sources of income) anywhere along the value chain into full-time equivalent positions.

In the case of agricultural raw materials such as tea and palm oil, the FTEs are based on a calculation of annual per capita labour productivity in plantation agriculture, divided into UI's use of that material. For cassava and coconut sugar, the calculations are based on the number of dedicated full-time producers required to produce the quantities of material used by UI. For black-soy production, the calculations are based on estimates of FTE labour used for black soy grown sequentially as one of three crops each year.

From this research it is clear that a very large and wide-ranging group of people are linked with UI's value chain. Many more individuals are linked with the chain than the FTE totals would suggest. For the majority of these people, their linkages with UI's value chain represent one of several diverse livelihood activities. Accordingly, the percentage of their total income that can be attributed to their links with UI may be quite small.

In the case of *warung* owners, for example, income from the *warung* represents around 42 per cent of household income. Income from sales of UI products represents about 10 per cent of the *warung* income. Assuming that there are some 551,000 *warungs* in Indonesia (this is a conservative figure; UI and others estimate that there may be as many as 1.8 million such enterprises), and assuming that — as our research suggests — each store supports three full-time equivalents, it is possible to suggest that the sale of UI products supports an estimated 10 per cent of 1,653,000 FTEs in small-scale retailing — or 165,300 FTEs.

This research cannot determine how much of this employment was generated by UI over and above employment levels that would have existed in the Indonesian economy if UI had not had operations there. Nor could the research determine net benefits in terms of increased incomes or savings for those in the value chain. But even though they are only indicative, the figures are still enlightening. This is particularly true for public-policy discussions among governments, CSOs, and businesses trying to compare labour-intensive industries with capital-intensive industries, or exploring industry structures that can offer benefits in training, credit, and other areas that are an integral part of being in the value chain of a company like UI.

Resources and share of value generated in the value chain

Most value-chain analysis of multinational companies has focused on employment generation as a proxy for income and equity, assuming that employment is a valid indicator of wages and income.

Another way to evaluate the impact of an FMCG company is to follow the price of a product from the production of the raw-material inputs of which it is made, through the various traders, processors, manufacturers, distributors, and ultimately to the consumer. This type of analysis is most often undertaken by companies who want to find ways to create greater efficiency within the value chain.

This kind of analysis is also promising in that it goes beyond employment generation to analyse the cumulative value of economic benefits for people in the value chain. Importantly, such analysis helps to identify key pressure points or leverage points for possible change through the value chain. This makes this type of analysis potentially far more useful in the design of pro-poor strategies than an emphasis on employment alone, and opens up for consideration non-income aspects of poverty such as education, skill development, and the power of poor people in markets.[31]

Figure 7 on page 83 estimates the value that is generated and distributed through wages as well as through the production and sale of raw materials and other input supplies, and by manufacturing, distribution, taxes, and retail sales of UI-manufactured and UI-branded products through UI's value chain. It is a summary estimate of the gross margins of most of the entities in UI's value chain, from the producers of raw materials to the retailers. This may be the first time that this type of information has been generated for the operations of any MNC, even in a single country. There has been no attempt to identify all the companies that derived economic benefit from an indirect relationship with the UI value chain. In addition, if there was not a good understanding of the value captured by different players in the system, their revenue streams or margins were not estimated in the figure.

The findings are significant. The total value generated by the UI value chain in Indonesia is conservatively estimated at Rp 5,431 billion (US$ 633 million). For its part, UI earns Rp 1,817 billion (US$ 212 million) before tax on the value that it creates as a key player in the value chain. The other entities in the value chain for whom estimates could be made (including taxes paid by UI to government) gained a combined Rp 3,614 billion (US$ 421 million), or about twice as much as UI. Strikingly, Figure 7 also shows that distributors and retailers gain a larger share of the total value than suppliers and producers (about 50 per cent more).

A comparison of the data as set out in Figure 6 and Figure 7 illustrates that the number of people touched by UI's value chain increases dramatically as one moves backwards or forwards along it. However, the percentage of the total income distributed by this 'touch' declines as it follows the value being added towards each end of the chain.

Figure 6: Estimated employment linked to UI's value chain (2003)

% of total employment linked to UI's value chain	Value-chain activity	Estimated jobs (FTEs)	% breakdown by category	
27.1	**Raw-material sourcing**	81,515	Cassava Palm oil Tea Coconut sugar Black soybeans	44 27 12 10 7
	Manufactured goods & other suppliers	24,000	Direct suppliers Indirect suppliers	33 67
8 2.4 7.3	**UI operations**	7,069	Direct & temporary employees Contract workers 3rd-party producers[a]	46 28 26
	UI distribution operations	21,860	UI distributors UI sub-distributors Sales promotion teams Ice-cream hawkers	48 18 13 21
55.2	**Retail operations**	166,320	UI-supplied shops UI-supplied *warungs*	1 99
Estimated number of jobs (FTEs[b])		**300,764**		

NB: This chart is an initial analysis of local research and data. It is the best estimate available at this time. Further work is necessary to categorise more precisely and allocate more accurately the precise job-multiplier impacts along the value chain.

a Excluding advertisers.

b FTE= full-time equivalent

Figure 7: Estimated distribution of value generated along UI's value chain (2003)[a]

% of total value generated	Value-chain activity	Rp billion	US$ million	% breakdown by category	
4[b]	Raw-material sourcing	232	27	Local raw materials	62
				Imported materials	38
12	Manufactured goods & other suppliers	638	74	Direct suppliers	54
				Indirect suppliers	25
				Advertising suppliers	21
34	UI operations	1,817	212	UI operating costs	69
				UI employees	26
				UI Indonesian shareholders	5
26	Taxes paid by UI	1,457	170	UI taxes[c]	100
6	UI distribution operations	332	39	UI distributors	93
				UI sub-distributors	7
18	Retail operations	955	111	UI shops and *warungs*	80
				Non-UI *warungs*	20
Estimated total value generated		**5,431**	**633**		

Notes

a Gross margins are defined as total sales revenues minus the cost of goods sold. By using estimates of the 'gross' margins for each participant in UI's value chain, this figure attempts to show how value is created and where it is captured along the entire chain for UI's products. The proxy we have used for gross margins for UI is profit before tax (US$ 212 million). (An alternative proxy could be Operating Income [$204 million], but that does not include interest income or foreign-exchange earnings.) Ten per cent is used as a proxy to calculate gross margins for raw-material suppliers, direct suppliers, and retailers. While the research for this report suggested that the gross margins for these value-chain participants vary between 5 and16 per cent, 10 per cent appears to be representative for each. These calculations are estimates. Further work is necessary to categorise and allocate more accurately the precise value added along the value chain.

b As primarily a home-care and personal-care company, only a small proportion of UI's product range uses agricultural raw materials.

c Excludes sales taxes.

Key insights: the value chain from supply to distribution

Supplier companies

UI's extensive purchases of goods and services through a local supply chain represent a major economic multiplier of UI's local investment. The company's investment in local suppliers ensures a steady supply of high-quality inputs and supports local jobs, profits, assets, and tax revenues. This strategy boosts the quality of local manufacturing, both through technical assistance programmes and the extension of UI's quality-management systems down the supply chain. This report gives examples of small and medium-sized local firms that have grown in partnership with UI. The company's top ten suppliers by value are all Indonesian. They account for 34 per cent of purchases and have supplied UI consistently for 15 years on average.

Compliance with stringent quality requirements can place heavy demands on supplier companies. However, the benefit for them may be a market with an agreed volume of sales at a guaranteed price, and the security of guaranteed payment where supplier goods meet UI's quality standards. Over the longer term, such relationships can improve the quality of domestic manufacturing in Indonesia. This can lead to sectoral expansion and associated increases in employment, profits, household and SME assets, and tax revenues, some of which will benefit poor people in the economy. All UI suppliers are required to observe Unilever's Code of Business Principles, which covers ethical, social, and environmental issues, including workers' rights. While pay and conditions among local supplier firms are generally less generous than within UI, the company maintains basic standards through negotiations, on-going dialogue, and a rolling three-year programme of auditing.

This project identified two aspects of UI's supply-chain operations and management that may have potentially negative impacts and provide an opportunity for further investigation and action. First, where supplier companies are using contract workers, there is an additional challenge to ensure that UI's standards are being met. Second, because UI purchases large volumes of inputs of manufactured and semi-manufactured goods from suppliers, it can negotiate lower prices. This pressure on prices may in turn be transferred back by the supplier to raw-material producers who are not in a position of strength from which to negotiate with the company or the traders that supply it.

Primary producers

One of the potential economic and social impacts of UI's presence in Indonesia is on local supply chains that reach directly to raw-materials producers for labour-intensive raw materials such as coconut sugar, palm oil, cassava, tea, and black soybeans. UI helps to create local markets for large numbers of local producers. But it does not automatically follow that local raw-materials producers benefit economically and socially from engaging in the supply chain, as the case of the coconut-sugar producers shows.

The UI black-soybean case suggests that alternative supply chains can bring benefits for both poor producers and the companies who buy from them. This secures for UI a consistent supply of high-quality raw materials and also reduces their purchasing costs. At the same time, such approaches, supported by large companies and their suppliers, can help small-scale farmers to benefit from markets that guarantee purchase volumes, prices, and delivery timing, as well as enabling them to obtain credit, technology transfer, and better prices for products. Thus, in some important respects, alternative supply-chain contracts can mitigate significant risks faced by small-scale producers. However, the research also indicated that the producers engaging in the alternative supply chain faced a new risk: that their crop might be rejected on the grounds of poor quality or late delivery.

New pro-poor initiatives to strengthen the market power of small-scale producers are required. Ideally these will combine the leadership of individual companies and industry-wide initiatives. Both are more likely to succeed if the business case is recognised by both companies and producers themselves, if it serves long-term business goals that are broader than cutting costs, and if change is supported by governments, CSOs, and consumers.

The distribution chain

The distribution chain for UI's products is complex. It consists of a mixture of wholesalers and 'modern' and 'traditional' retailers and vendors, and it extends to street hawkers selling ice cream. It is clear from this study that a large number of livelihoods throughout Indonesia are supported within this chain. There are full-time and part-time jobs in wholesale distributor companies and retailers, including those who own or work in grocery stores, *warungs,* kiosks, and street vending operations. In fact, UI supports more employment generation and value generation on the distribution side of the value chain than it does on the supply side.

As with the supply chain, the closer that distributors and modern retailers are in the chain to UI, the more likely they are to gain skills and knowledge, and experience higher employment standards, higher incomes, and the ability to build up business capital. At the very edge of the formal economy, where small retail activities can represent a large portion of family income, both incomes and standards of product handling and storage tend to be lower. To an even greater extent than the supply chain, the local 'multiplier' impact of the distribution chain is little understood, and its role in helping poor people become established in the formal economy needs further exploration.

Initiatives such as smaller-sized product packages of consumer goods, which are more accessible to low-income consumers, support employment through the distribution system. So even if a product does not have a particularly large impact on employment or incomes on the supply side, it can still have such impacts through distribution. Whether and how UI or other large companies could further contribute to economic development for small-scale retailers is an area for further study.

The overall value chain

Perhaps the most significant insight of this research was the importance of taking into consideration the overall value chain of a company, the cash-value distribution, and jobs supported within it, when exploring poverty impacts. Although estimates are only indicative, the research suggests that more than 300,000 full-time equivalent jobs are supported by UI's value chain – far more than the FTEs, totalling approximately 5,000, in UI's core workforce. Notably, around twice as many FTEs are linked with retailing and distribution as with primary production in UI's value chain. This report clearly illustrates that most of the value created by a FMCG company like UI is captured in its manufacturing, distribution, and retail sectors.

Participants at either end of the value chain are predominantly large numbers of small-scale producers and retailers. For them, UI's value chain provides an opportunity to participate in the formal economy, gaining skills and experience while supplementing and diversifying their incomes.

However, participation in such value chains does not automatically guarantee improvements in the lives of people living in poverty. For supply and distribution chains to benefit poor people even more, there need to be other social institutions and resources in place, such as credit and saving schemes, marketing associations, and insurance schemes, as well as diversification of income streams to reduce dependency on any single company or market.

Understanding and responding to this analysis represents an opportunity for companies, governments, and CSOs to explore how to distribute benefits further in each direction along the value chain, particularly to the poorest people who are working at the very ends of it. For Unilever, this is a question of how each participant can, sustainably, add more value, and so gain more benefit from their part in the chain, given the competitive markets in which FMCG companies operate. For Oxfam, the value captured by people working at the ends of the value chain, especially by primary producers at the supply end, will increase only where they have a stronger negotiating position in relation to their product or service, or where value chains are restructured to change the distribution of benefits. Whether or not there are additional ways for FMCG companies to work more directly and beneficially with each end of the value chain is an area that requires further research.

5 Low-income consumers in the marketplace

This chapter explores the position of poor people as consumers in developing countries. This was one of the most closely debated aspects of this project. Relating to people as consumers, including poor people as consumers, is at the heart of UI's business, but it is a relatively new topic for Oxfam to examine at this level of detail. Also it is one that generally has been little researched around the world, especially with an emphasis on poverty impacts.[32] For Oxfam, the opportunity to undertake research with a leading FMCG company, with an explicit and sophisticated strategy for marketing to people living in poverty, was an unusual and important opportunity to explore these issues.

For this project, a review of secondary data, company records, and 120 interviews with low-income consumers led the project team to identify and select some key issues to be considered. The issues selected for focus were as follows:

* Access to UI products, including who buys them, pricing and market share.
* The role of brands in the marketplace.
* The role of promotion and advertising.
* The extent to which companies are meeting or creating needs.

A study of UI's role and impact in the market reveals that constant change is a common theme, as the company continually responds to the development of consumer-goods markets to serve an increasingly urban population. Fast-moving consumer-goods markets are highly dynamic. The market in Indonesia is currently in one phase of development, but it will quickly develop and change as consumers' lifestyles evolve, and they experiment with new choices and make increasingly informed purchasing decisions. A company like UI may be a small or large player in a particular product category at different points in time, depending on changes in consumer demand. At each stage, companies face challenges which may necessitate trade-offs between financial and non-financial goals.

The debate about the ethical and social implications of extending FMCG markets to people living on limited financial resources is contentious and not easily resolved. It revolves around some basic questions about wants and needs, whether there is a 'right' way for consumers in general to spend their money, and to what extent consumer choice is unduly influenced by advertising. This chapter describes the outcome of exploring these issues in a spirit of enquiry and partnership.

The fast-moving consumer-goods (FMCG) market in Indonesia

International FMCG companies are increasingly reaching out to people living on low incomes around the world. They are marketing and selling goods that people need or want, across a range of income levels. The result is an increase in the worldwide consumer base for FMCG companies, and an increased use of branded goods by people living in poverty.

A number of factors, including a product's functionality, its perceived quality and value, the intensity of advertising and promotion, and the degree of competition that the product faces, affect the success of any consumer-goods product in the marketplace. Within Indonesia, FMCG markets are highly competitive and dynamic. Before the 1997 economic crisis they were already highly diversified, and they have continued to diversify even more since then. For example, in 1996 some 400 Indonesian cosmetics companies were registered with the Association of Cosmetics Companies. By 2004, there were 744 companies registered, including approximately 50 multinationals, 200 medium-sized companies, and about 500 small companies.[33] Within these markets, UI's brands remain popular. UI has more than 50 per cent market share of some product categories such as ice cream, margarine, toothpaste, hair care, and fabric conditioner. Other UI products do not have such a large share of the market: for example, UI's culinary and seasonings products have a market share of less than 3 per cent.

For the most part, the recent proliferation of FMCG companies appears to have resulted from increased overall consumption, linked in part to shifts in population from rural to urban areas, and increased market penetration generally. However, the consumption rate of many consumer-goods products is still fairly low in Indonesia. For example, per capita consumption of toothpaste is 200 g per person per year in Indonesia – only 10 per cent of the level in Singapore, according to the ASEAN Cosmetic Association. If the Indonesian economy continues to grow, consumption generally will increase, including in FMCG markets.

What exactly does UI sell?

Unilever Indonesia sells a range of home-care and personal-care (HPC) items and food products that are attractive to consumers of all income levels, including people living in poverty. The full product range is listed in Appendix 2. In 2003, around 84 per cent of UI total sales were HPC, and 16 per cent were foods. In the same year, UI's home and personal care business grew by 14 per cent, while the foods business, including ice cream, grew by 28 per cent.

UI products fall into three broad categories:

- *Personal-care products*, such as soap (Lux, Lifebuoy), oral care (Close-Up, Pepsodent), shampoo (Sunsilk, Clear, Lifebuoy), skin care (Dove, Vaseline, Ponds Citra), and deodorant (Rexona, Axe). UI also sells tissues, baby diapers, and feminine-care products.

- *Household-cleaning materials and detergents*, such as clothes-washing detergent (Omo, Sunlight, Rinso, Surf) and home-cleaning products (Domestos Nomos, Sunlight, Vim).

- *Food products*, such as margarine (Blue Band), tea (Sariwangi, Lipton), seasonings and sauces (Royco, Kecap Bango), ice cream (Walls), and other food 'treats'.

Who buys UI products?

According to UI data, 95 per cent of households in Indonesia use at least one UI product.[34] UI targets consumers from all market segments, and its products are purchased by all socio-economic groups.

In the limited research undertaken for this report, interviews suggested that the average poor family spends 5.7 per cent of its average monthly out-goings on UI products. Data show that people living on lower incomes spend a greater proportion of their budget on FMCGs than those who have larger incomes. Those with less cash in hand still choose to purchase personal care and cleaning products, as well as food brands. These goods are often bought on a daily basis in small sachets or pouches.

Most poor consumers throughout Indonesia buy UI products in *warungs* or from market stalls in their neighbourhoods. Research for this project found that typical low-income consumers shopping in *warungs* tend to be married women in their thirties, with three or more children. These are the people responsible for making most household purchases. *Warungs* tend to stock a mix of manufactured and branded items, as well as bulk items and fresh produce.

Access to UI products

The research work and UI data provided some valuable insights into constraints on poor people's access to UI products.

Many of UI's product sales in Indonesia represent basic goods, such as hand-washing soap, laundry products, and tea. In the FMCG industry a number of factors might constrain access to such goods, including pricing and geographical access to retailers selling the products.

Product pricing

People living in poverty are not only disadvantaged by low wages and prices for the agricultural and other goods that they produce: they may also have to pay high prices for foodstuffs and other essentials, which reduce the value of their (already low) incomes. As noted earlier, households in Indonesia are thought on average to be spending 60 per cent of their income on food, beverages, and tobacco products, which means that prices for such products are of great importance to them.

Table 10 illustrates UI's recommended retail prices (RRP) for a range of popular products, compared with some household staples such as rice.

Keeping prices low makes UI products more affordable for low-income consumers. An important part of UI's low-price strategy is the availability of everyday products in small sachets. There are social and environmental issues associated with this strategy, which are discussed further below.

Table 10: UI products: price of smallest available units, compared with some household staples and popular products

Product/brand	Recommended retail price (RRP) (Rp) (2004)	Recommended retail price (RRP) (US$ equivalent) (2004)
Rice (1 kg)	2,900	0.34
Cooking oil (branded 250 ml bottle)	1,900	0.22
Coca-Cola (returnable bottle)	2,000	0.24
Clove cigarette (1 as priced on the street)	500	0.06
UI products		
Seasoning (Royco, 3.5g)	200	0.03
House-cleaning liquid (Super Pell, 25ml sachet)	250	0.03
Fabric conditioner (Molto Pewangi, 30ml sachet)	300	0.04
Shampoo (Lifebuoy, 6ml sachet)	350	0.04
Shampoo (Sunsilk, 6ml)	350	0.04
Laundry bleach (Sunclin, 40ml sachet)	350	0.04
Fabric wash (Rinso Anti Noda, 32g sachet)	400	0.05
Fabric wash (Surf, 45g)	500	0.06
Tea (Sariwangi, 5x1.85g teabags in a pack)	500	0.06
Toothpaste (Pepsodent, 25g)	1,000	0.12
Fabric wash (Surf, 100g)	1,000	0.12
Soap (Lifebuoy 90g)	1,300	0.15
Soap (Lux 100g)	1,400	0.16
Soy sauce (Bango, 110ml)	1,500	0.18
Ice cream (Paddle Pop, 65ml)	1,700	0.20
Toothbrush (Pepsodent)	1,750	0.21
Mosquito coil (Domestos Nomos 5DC 60 box)	1,800	0.21

Market share and prices

Oxfam and CSOs are concerned about the risk that prices of basic products will increase if a small number of companies gain dominant market shares over time or in one geographic area, thus crowding out competition that helps to keep prices down. It has already been noted that the FMCG industry in Indonesia generally is highly competitive. Some UI brands are leaders within a category, such as ice cream, toothpaste, and hair care. These brand leaders tend to be at the premium end of the product category, consumed by social groups with marginally higher incomes, particularly urban groups. However, in a key category such as powder detergents, international companies UI and Kao face very strong competition from large, locally owned companies such as Wings Surya (which also competes in toothpaste and hair-care products) and Sinar Antjol.

A related question of importance for Oxfam and CSOs is whether the entry of large international companies into local markets leads to displacement of small-scale local producers. It is true in many cases that large companies like UI enter product lines and markets with substantial resources for marketing and distribution; they also benefit from economies of scale and thus can offer lower prices. However, UI is very active in supporting SMEs who are both suppliers to and customers for UI brands. Oxfam strongly endorses the view that a good industrial policy for developing countries includes nurturing the ability of independent small producers, whether non-branded or using their own brand, to compete successfully with global brands in the local marketplace. While such competition exists in FMCG markets in Indonesia, from the research it was difficult to judge the overall balance of market share between international and locally owned businesses across the wide range of products provided by the industry.

Both UI and Oxfam recognise that competition benefits consumers by reducing prices and raising product standards over time. Oxfam believes that it is important for diversity of both local and global brands to continue to exist in the marketplace – because this competition is good for the local economy and for consumers. UI has many local FMCG competitor companies of various sizes. For example, when UI entered the soap market in Indonesia in the 1930s, the market was estimated at 80,000 MT. By 2004, it was 675,000 MT, with a range of local and international competitors engaged in production. This market growth was due in part to UI's investment in advertising to raise consumer awareness about washing with soap, which developed the market for soap overall, not solely for UI products.

Price variation

Indonesia is a huge country of 6,000 inhabited islands, covering two million square kilometres from the Indian Ocean to the Pacific. The country's geography poses great challenges to companies endeavouring to establish distribution networks to reach consumers everywhere across the nation. Transportation costs are a particular challenge. As a result, consumers living on distant islands or in isolated rural areas often find prices significantly higher than the recommended retail price. The research found that through innovations and efficiencies in its distribution network, UI has been able to avoid increasing its prices to wholesalers and retailers on the grounds of distance, and instead maintains the same uniform RRP for its products across the nation.

Several factors outside the control of UI affect the price that a consumer pays for goods. Very important is the fact that low-income consumers tend to buy their products from local shops or *warungs*, which are more conveniently located. Research undertaken for this report showed that in many cases the actual sale prices in a local shop are different from the RRP – in some lower, and in some higher. In some cases, the *warung* price paid for products is between 20 and nearly 50 per cent higher than UI's recommended retail price. For example, the cost of a 6 ml sachet of Clear was 43 per cent higher than at the supermarket, where it was sold for the Recommended Selling Price of Rp 350. Similarly, the price of Pepsodent toothpaste (75 gm) was 6 per cent higher in the *warung* than the UI Recommended Selling Price.[35]

One reason for this price difference is retailer mark-ups of 10 to 20 per cent to cover transport and storage costs, and the involvement of middlemen, wholesalers, and the retailers themselves. An additional reason for this problem is that retailers find it difficult to charge UI's Recommended Retail Price and provide small change, given that there are few single-rupiah coins. So most retailers round up the price of the product. UI has tried to address this issue by adjusting the weight of the sachet contents – but without success, because the *warung* owners adjust their prices upwards again to match convenient price points.

However in some cases, shoppers at some *warungs* pay less for products than at other shops. This occurs when *warung* owners purchase goods in bulk at supermarkets or hypermarkets, and the prices are lower than those used by UI distributors.

Why do people buy UI products? The concept of brands

In spite of the economic crisis, UI has consistently gained market share. This is due to a number of factors, but five guiding principles stand out as relevant to this project:

- providing good value for money;
- establishing an effective wide-scale distribution network (as described in Chapter 4);
- paying close attention to consumer needs and wants;
- marketing brands effectively;
- marketing small, affordable sachet sizes of relatively expensive branded goods.

Detailed consumer research conducted by UI during the economic crisis of the late 1990s revealed that consumers prioritise *value* for the money that they spend, not *cheapness*. A low-income consumer cannot afford to make purchasing mistakes, for example by buying non-effective products. In addition, low-income consumers require package sizes that are commensurate with their daily cash-in-hand limitations. Most importantly, UI discovered among both urban and rural buyers a universal unwillingness to compromise on quality of daily-use products: 'low income' consumers still want to buy quality products and will endeavour to do so if their financial means allow it. A brand is perceived to guarantee a certain quality of performance, in preference to the alternative of buying an unbranded product of potentially variable quality.

The project research suggested that most low-income consumers in Indonesia perceive UI products to be more expensive than other brands, but more than half said that they would buy more if they had more money. Even low-income consumers perceive UI products to be superior to non-UI products. The response from this small research sample mirrors the findings of UI's own marketing research.

In response to criticism by CSOs and others that brands generally, and international brands in particular, threaten diversity of products in the marketplace, Unilever replies that it sets global standards on critical safety issues for products and ingredients, taking into account all product-development work, no matter where it takes place in the world. Since consumers all around the world are eating Unilever products and using them on their bodies, these standards are often higher than those required by local law. For example, UI does not use ingredients such as lead acetate in hair-blackening products, even though they are permitted in both Indonesia and the EU, because the company prefers to use more benign alternatives. Similarly, in its detergent products UI uses surfactants that are rapidly and completely biodegradable, although use of less expensive, slow-biodegrading alternatives is still permitted by law.

Box 9: The views of Unilever and Oxfam on the role of a brand

For Unilever, a brand is in effect the first step in consumer protection, because it puts the producer's 'mark' clearly on the product for all to see. A brand is a guarantee of quality and consistency, giving assurance that 'what you bought last time is what you will get next time'. It is about trust. It enables people to think: 'This brand will always give me what I expect'. Consumers need to have a product that does exactly what it says on the label. Unilever believes this is just as important today in Indonesia as it was when it first began mass-marketing branded soap in Victorian England.

For Oxfam, brands are the basis for building a set of attributes – both tangible and intangible – associated with a product, and hence forming the basis for advertising. While advertising can provide valuable information about a product, Oxfam believes that most advertisements go far beyond conveying factual information. By shaping consumers' wants and needs, and portraying the use of a product by people with aspirational lifestyles, advertising creates the intangible brand attribute of 'being like them'.

Evidence shows that social marketing campaigns can shift consumer demand towards healthier choices. This demonstrates how powerful advertising can be in changing behaviour. But social messages do not usually have the financial backing equivalent to commercial product marketing. In this sense, while competing brands appear to present consumers with choices, the choices presented are not always neutral, complete, or made with full information.

In Indonesia, most products sold in small stores and *warungs* are branded products produced by large local and international companies. Yet in most of UI's product categories, local, low-cost, un-branded alternatives do exist. Nevertheless, Oxfam is concerned that the availability of these local alternatives is declining over time, because smaller companies producing them lack the sophisticated packaging, distribution, and promotion mechanisms that big companies have. Food items are of particular concern to Oxfam, which believes that the expansion of large FMCG companies could potentially have the most negative impact on established local food producers and manufacturers, by displacing them in the marketplace. Citing its experience and research, UI takes a different view and says that at the end of the day it is the consumer who chooses. Just as in Western markets, if a brand loses touch with its consumers, they will change their spending patterns.

The role of promotion and advertising

Like most FMCG companies, UI advertises in order to develop and maintain brand awareness, to launch new products, and remain competitive within the Indonesian market. UI is one of the biggest advertisers in Indonesia, employing sophisticated marketing techniques to reach consumers. In 2003 UI spent approximately 12 per cent of net sales on advertising (AC Nielsen AdSpend Survey 2003). A total of 1,940,859 million Rp (US$ 226 million) was spent on all aspects of marketing and selling, including some distribution and other costs, including depreciation. A total of 1,271,508 million Rp (US$ 148 million), or 15.6 per cent of net sales, was spent on 'advertising, promotion and research' (UI Annual Report 2003), which includes promotions, trade incentives, merchandising, and market research.

UI's spending on advertising increased by 36 per cent between 2002 and 2003, with the largest increase being in television advertising (40 per cent) (Nielson Media Research AdQuest 2003). Some of the company's brands are promoted more extensively than others. The advertising and promotions budget for a new brand can be as high as 50 per cent of its net sales. For existing brands, the ratio is only 10–15 per cent; between 2002 and 2003, spending on advertising for Sunsilk shampoo declined from Rp 144 billion to Rp 115 billion, or 20 per cent. Eighty-nine per cent of advertising is for global brands such as Sunsilk and Pepsodent, and 11 per cent for Indonesian brands such as Kecap Bango and Sariwangi tea.[36] UI aims to ensure that it advertises in a responsible way, in accordance with its worldwide brand-communication principles. According to UI, the company pays particular attention to local cultural differences and perceptions, and the need to produce advertisements with local-language variations around consistent themes and branding positions. A great deal of advertising is generated or adapted by local Indonesian agencies.

Between 2002 and 2003, UI spending on advertising for Pond's skin-lightening cream doubled from Rp 46 billion to Rp 97 billion. In 2003, UI spent 72 per cent more than in the previous year to advertise Rinso detergent and Lifebuoy soap. A key factor for UI in determining advertising spend is what its competitors are doing with their brands. Spending on the detergent Surf more than doubled, from Rp 38 billion to Rp 92 billion. However, Wings Surya, the local market leader, outspends UI on advertising its own powder detergents (AC Nielsen AdSpend Survey 2003).

Oxfam and other CSOs believe that the branded products of MNCs and their local operations, such as UI, as well as some large domestic companies, such as Wings Surya, gain market share through advertising, leading to a displacement of smaller domestic producers. Oxfam is concerned that these trends may lead in the long term to reduced choice, at a cost to the consumer. It believes that smaller domestic companies may be losing power to multinational and large national brands, as they are unable to compete in the face of well-financed advertising messages for FMCG products that obtain blanket coverage in the media – especially television – and public spaces. While this project did not focus on research that would be necessary to conclude whether UI's presence in Indonesia has displaced smaller local producers of other competing products, Oxfam argues that local entrepreneurs cannot compete with MNCs when it comes to advertising budgets and the ability to use 'loss leaders' to subsidise new product lines. This remains an open question, as does the degree to which local producers are in fact able to grow by developing local variants of new products for which markets have been developed by international companies.

In Unilever's experience, branded goods tend to promote competition, which benefits the consumer by increasing access to quality products and reducing prices over time. UI suggests that the company's investment in growing the market for quality soap and cleaning products, in particular, has led to increased consumer demand for these products, and thus more opportunity for domestic players. In turn this increases demand for raw materials and thus for suppliers.

Oxfam is concerned, too, about the amount of money spent on advertising to change consumers' spending patterns to branded products. At the equivalent of around 11 per cent of net sales, advertising, promotions, and other market-development costs are factors in consumer prices. In the research for this project, it was evident that some consumers realised this, while others were unaware that advertising costs were increasing the prices of branded products. The research was not designed to lead to conclusions regarding whether or not the level of spending on advertising and promotions was appropriate, particularly when it would need to be compared with UI's competitors in the marketplace.

While advertising is an essential communication tool for UI, the company adopts various other forms of communications with consumers (see Box 10 on page 96).

Meeting or creating needs?

In his book, *The Fortune at the Bottom of the Pyramid*, C.K. Prahalad sets out a strong case for the potential of companies to expand markets in poor countries. He contends that people living in poverty want, and have a right to share in, the types of basic product that are widely available in developed countries. FMCG companies like UI believe that marketing to the poor is just as important as marketing to the wealthy, because it is responding to a demand. People living in poverty with little disposable income also want to have high-quality personal-care products, clean clothes, and safe food. UI notes that it is providing goods that are desired and, many would argue, needed.

UI views most of its products as basic, or even essential, requirements for everyday living. Detergents and soap are relevant to basic health care: clean homes, clean clothes, and hand-washing play an important role in preventing disease. Personal grooming plays a role in establishing personal self-esteem, and even people living in poverty celebrate important events with some form of 'reward' or 'treat'. UI aims to tailor its food and drink products to suit the tastes and lifestyles of Indonesian families, including everyday goods like tea and soup stock, as well as 'treat' products like ice-cream.

However, for Oxfam there remains the question of how a product can be defined as basic or essential when, for poor households, it means purchasing less of something else that is essential for the well-being of the household, like health care or education. In other words, for every purchase there is an 'opportunity cost' of not purchasing something else. Oxfam questions whether it is appropriate to market FMCGs aggressively to people living on limited budgets. Advertising runs the risk of turning 'luxuries' into necessities, both at the household level and across communities, at the expense of more important goods and services. Do consumers meet their

Box 10: Communications between UI and consumers

UI is actively engaged in dialogue with consumers in Indonesia. Consumers can contact UI directly to express their views on UI brands. On average, they contact UI 2,500 times per month, mostly by telephone (UI provides a toll-free telephone number), letter, and email. The feedback falls into four general categories: inquiries (44 per cent), complaints (37 per cent), compliments (13 per cent), and suggestions (6 per cent). The company reports that 95 per cent of complaints are answered within the time prescribed by the company. In addition it receives informa-tion from Sales Push Teams: company and distributor sales forces who meet consumers and listen to them directly every day.

This personal daily contact between consumers, their retailers, and UI distribution people is the source of the most accessible, regular feedback of consumer opinion on the company's brands. Any fall in sales is a signal that consumer opinion about a brand, for whatever reason, is changing, and the decline is investigated to understand the reasons behind the changes in consumers' purchasing decisions.

In the research for this report, 23 of the 120 consumers interviewed indicated that they had concerns about some of the UI products that they had used; typically these were individuals' opinions about products. None had ever made a complaint to the company. So UI's consumer helpline may not be so effective for poor consumers who do not have telephones, or who may be uncomfortable using them to voice complaints.

families' needs before purchasing more luxury items? It is important to consider – but difficult to measure – to what extent advertising shapes, rather than responds to, consumer values and demand, creating dependency on branded products and eroding cultural values and norms.

Most of UI's products sold in Indonesia are personal-care and cleaning products, sold at affordable prices. But Oxfam has concerns about advertising for products without clear benefits for nutrition or hygiene, such as snack foods like ice-cream and personal products like skin-lightening cream. UI maintains that both markets pre-dated the company's entry, and that the provision of good-quality and safe alternatives performs a useful function.

There is anecdotal evidence that advertising through the mass media, particularly on TV, is shaping local culture. In the small survey of consumers conducted for this report, children, unlike their parents, seem to have strong brand preferences. Half of the parents surveyed had no objections regarding those preferences, while 30 per cent had some objections. This is an important issue for many pro-poor and consumer groups, who believe that advertising creates and encourages 'pester' power (children begging parents for popular products when they go on shopping trips together), and that this does not result in the best use of money to improve the diet or hygiene of children in low-income families.

While the research approach was to ask people living in poverty about impacts on their lives, the sample size was far smaller than that of the extensive market-survey work regularly undertaken by UI, and the project team was unable to agree conclusions about the impact on poor people of purchasing UI's products. The research and data provided by UI were more helpful in addressing some questions than others, particularly where major conceptual issues need to be clarified and better understood.

Case study 4: Small sachets: a response to consumer demands

As discussed, UI survived the economic crisis of 1997–98 by means of a strategy that enabled the company to remain competitive. One key factor in UI's success was innovative initiatives to ensure that consumers continued to value and use UI products. UI's response was to expand the use of low-priced sachets of several of its products, specifically for consumers with limited cash. Basic products such as Sunsilk shampoo and Rinso detergent are available in sachets, and foods such as Kecap Bango in small pouches. Small sachet packets now account for most sales of UI products such as shampoos.

The company needed to keep its products available to consumers whose spending power was daily decreasing as inflation rose. The term 'low-income consumers' described an increasingly large proportion of the population as the Indonesian currency lost value.

In interviews carried out for this research, low-income consumers reported choosing products for their taste and quality. Sales figures and surveys of consumer demand suggest that consumers want the opportunity to buy quality products in smaller packages at lower prices. They buy goods at varied intervals, from once a day (Clear brand shampoo, for example) to once a week (Sariwangi tea bags). Their perception is that products in sachets or small pouches are affordable and more practical.

While these consumers understand that buying products in larger quantities would save them money, since the cost per unit is lower, they choose the small sachets because they are thus enabled to obtain the products with small amounts of money as and when they have the cash. Low-income consumers interviewed insisted they would be happy to buy more simply packaged sachets, provided that the price was reduced commensurately and the quality was maintained. Oxfam argues that small sachet products, while more affordable, *are not more economical.* Indeed, smaller-size packages incur higher costs per unit of product for the consumer, for the shop selling them, and even for the company making them.

From an environmental point of view, the popularity of small packages among consumers raises some challenges. Small packages require more plastic. As UI makes its products more affordable to low-income consumers, it generates larger amounts of packaging waste, which pollute the environment. According to the research in poor communities, sachets are burned as rubbish, disposed of on common land in the village, or thrown into rivers. Farmers growing organic rice noted that those who burn the plastic can no longer use their household ash as a fertiliser, because it damages their crops.

Unilever is investigating different means of improving consumer disposal of packaging. It uses polyethylene terephthalate (PET), a plastic widely used in food and drink packaging. PET is categorised as non-toxic, and therefore classified as non-harmful when disposed of. The difficulty lies at least in part in segregating the different types of material that end up on a village rubbish heap. The findings here indicate the need for further assessment. UI is piloting a 'Litter Bug' recycling project, in which the company is working together with rubbish collectors and supporting small-scale converters to recycle the plastic waste into household products such as plastic bags, mats, and sandals. However, the financial incentive to collect and recycle the plastic waste is still very limited and is successful only on a very small scale, near recycling plants.

Key insights: low-income consumers in the marketplace

Recent years have seen an increase in the worldwide consumer base for MNCs, and an increased use of branded goods by people living in poverty. The debate about extending FMCG markets to people living on limited financial resources is contentious and not easily resolved. It revolves around some basic questions about wants and needs, whether there is a 'right' way for poor people and consumers in general to spend their money, and to what extent consumer choice is unduly influenced by advertising.

The project research suggested that consumers living in poverty may choose to prioritise value for money over cheapness. While Unilever and UI products may not always be the cheapest brands available, they are often perceived by low-income consumers to be more effective than competing brands, and many consumers will endeavour to purchase them whenever possible. In addition, UI's approach to selling goods in smaller sachets, developed during the financial crisis, has provided poor consumers with a more flexible purchasing option which, although a more costly approach to purchasing over the long term, reflects their day-to-day cash-in-hand limitations. For UI, low-income consumers' preferences for Unilever products are confirmation of the guarantee of consistent quality that the Unilever brands provide. Oxfam supports approaches that enable low-income consumers to obtain good-quality essential products at affordable prices, but also acknowledges that the impacts of marketing on consumer preferences are complex, and that the development of consumer preferences may be the result of intangible brand attributes and not solely of objective 'facts' about products.

Marketing to people living in poverty has clear benefits for poor people when certain conditions are met: for example, when products represent good value for money, or when they serve poverty-related social or environmental goals. Both Oxfam and Unilever are interested in finding ways for companies to meet these conditions. One clear way to do this in the FMCG sector is to promote better hygiene through use of hand-washing soap. Other opportunities exist, and insofar as UI and other companies can address them, they can have positive impacts that go beyond the companies' own financial success. For example, marketing to people living in poverty can serve their interests in the following circumstances:

- If it gives them access to high-quality products that are good for health or well-being more generally.
- If it improves the value of their limited disposable income.
- If product choice and competition between brands lead to lower prices, or consumers are provided with better information about products.
- If it increases economic opportunities in their communities by creating jobs in the distribution network or the supply chain: in particular, jobs that provide working capital or new types of skill and opportunity.
- If it spreads new technology or product ideas that local producers can adapt and use.

In the time available it was impossible to assess the extent to which the impacts listed above are being achieved by UI's marketing, but the research did help the project team to define more clearly the types of indicator that governments, companies, and CSOs could use to explore the issues further.

6 UI's wider impact in the community

This chapter explores UI's wider impacts in the community, in particular focusing on UI's voluntary community contributions, and the company's influence on the government and on other companies operating in Indonesia.

Research for this chapter included interviews with people living close to UI facilities, and information provided by UI. The company's influence on the business sector and government was not explored in depth, and no new research was undertaken into these impacts.

Corporate community involvement

Oxfam and many other CSOs urge companies to focus more attention and resources on changing the 'poverty footprint' of their core business practices, rather than focusing on philanthropy. Unilever agrees that its greatest social impacts are felt through its mainstream operations, and so the research behind this project focused mostly on the value chain, rather than on UI's voluntary community contributions. However, it is important to note that corporate philanthropy and involvement in community development can also play a role in a company's long-term contribution to the community. In turn there are benefits for the company. The line that defines what is acceptable corporate philanthropy and what is product promotion or an overt business strategy may vary from one country to another. Examples of UI's philanthropy, its other community-based initiatives, and the experiences of some communities living close to UI facilities are highlighted to show the range of ways in which MNCs like UI can have impact on the wider community.

The researchers interviewed a number of communities living within one kilometre of UI facilities. Of those interviewed, half claimed to receive a direct benefit from UI's presence in their community. These benefits included direct employment, increased commerce and sales in local shops, increased passengers for motorbike taxis, and opportunities to maintain or repair the bicycles or motorbikes of UI employees.

Examples of UI traditional philanthropy

UI's traditional philanthropic activities, intended to benefit communities, include the following:

- **Peduli Foundation:** in November 2000, the PT UI Peduli Foundation (UI Care Foundation) was created and financed with Rp 10 billion (US$ 1 million) 'to revitalize corporate social responsibility and sustainable development as part of its branding image'. In 2003, UI supported some 40 organisations with total contributions worth approximately Rp 11.3 billion;[37] about 70 per cent of this support was given as in-kind contributions, and about 30 per cent in cash. The Foundation also invested in projects that 'helped it make a difference in addressing the crisis situation by taking a leadership role in promoting CSR to other companies in Indonesia'.[38]

- **SME Composting Program:** UI acts in partnership with an NGO and local government in Karah, Kecamatan Jambangan, Surabaya to support village-level composting. Organic waste is composted into fertiliser and soil enhancers, and the inorganic wastes are sold to recyclers. This project has reduced overall waste, demonstrated the value of composting, and reduced the need to purchase soil enhancers. It has also generated employment and income.

- **Sustainable Clean Rivers Development Program:** UI supports efforts to reduce water pollution in the Brantas River, the second-largest river in Java. The goal is to reduce the volumes of waste water and garbage that are dumped in the river, to improve local sanitation, to change the local lifestyles that produce pollution, and to manage wastes. The programme also helps families to increase their incomes through the production or processing of medicinal plants.

- **Promoting Sustainable Fishing Practice:** UI has signed a memorandum of understanding (MOU) with World Wide Fund for Nature (WWF) Indonesia to promote better fisheries management, especially on tropical reef fisheries that are not sustainably managed.

Examples of community involvement with financial benefits for UI

UI also works on community-based initiatives, such as small-business development and consumer education, which bring indirect and direct benefits to the business. Some examples of this include the following:

- A donation of US$ 200,000 to UNICEF from UI in 1999 enabled the re-opening of 900 health centres that had been closed during the crisis, when public funding was cut. In these health centres the company placed free samples of soap, leaflets, and public-service advertisements to help to reduce the incidence of diarrhoea and intestinal worms.

- After the 1997 financial crisis, the Indonesian government abandoned family-planning programmes in rural areas. For an interim period,

UI stepped in and provided financial assistance to keep more than 200 people engaged in this work. UI arranged for family-planning staff to sell its products door to door in rural areas and receive a commission on sales, at the same time as performing their professional duties.

- UI has several initiatives to educate consumers about health care and hygiene. These include dental health-care programmes and free dental check-ups. The company also gives scholarships for high-achieving university students whose families cannot afford their fees.

- UI helped to expand the processing capacity of Subang Fish Sauce Supplier, a local fish-sauce supplier, and has agreed to defer outstanding loans for operational costs to accommodate the expansion.

The UI Peduli Foundation Project SMALL is an example of UI corporate philanthropy that can also be seen as an investment which benefits UI in the long term. In 2000, the Foundation set up Project SMALL to give Indonesians with no established business networks or connections the chance to become entrepreneurs. Bringing into play its own knowledge and skills base, UI increasingly saw that its community involvement could be more effective when linked to opportunities presented by the company's core business — for example, as a purchaser of raw materials, manufactured inputs, and finished products; as a contractor of service companies; and as a seller of retail products.

In 2001, UI signed a MOU with Indonesia's Department of Industry and Trade to support the creation of SME start-ups, as well as networks of SMEs to service them. Project SMALL provides entrepreneurs with market access, support, technical skills, and access to finance. IPPM (Institut Pendidikan dan Pengembangan Manajemen / Institute of Education and Management Development) provides technical skills and expertise in the food and catering business, identifying prospective entrepreneurs and locations, helping to build capacity, and helping new SMEs to obtain licences.

UI's influence on the business sector and government

The impacts of multinational companies are not limited to their employment practices or the products that they buy and sell. A potentially profound impact is their effect on the business culture within the country – whether by their commercial relationships with their own partners and stakeholders, or by their influence on peer companies or competitors. Another potential impact is the influence exerted by MNCs on government, either in terms of the regulatory context within which all companies operate, or in terms of policies on taxes, tariffs, or broader trade issues.

As a FMCG company, UI's relations and level of transactions with government agencies are not so great as those of MNCs in other sectors (such as extractive industries or infrastructure). UI's direct and indirect contribution to public-policy development includes its work through trade associations, for example to set standards for ingredients of cosmetics. UI believes that its track record and long-term commitment to Indonesia gives it credibility, influence, and responsibility throughout society. According to UI officials, the government offers UI as an example of a company which stayed in the country even when the overall investment climate was not optimal.

Doing business in Indonesia presents many challenges. As in many other countries, the use of non-transparent activities and influence to agree business deals is widespread. UI is committed to avoiding such practices throughout all of its operations, focusing rather on using policies and contracts to guide its interactions with government officials and other businesses. More work is needed to increase understanding of how UI's approach to doing business affects the smaller businesses in its supply chain, and their employees.

UI's influence in the wider business community and society in Indonesia is also seen in its relations with its business partners. As noted in previous chapters, UI requires its partners to obey the law, and recommends that they go further than the law requires in matters such as good workplace policies and practices.

A company can also influence peer companies (including competitors) in terms of business ethics, CSR, or overall business strategies. The best example of UI's potential contribution to influencing the behaviour of its peers is its work on corruption. For example, the NGO Transparency International asked the UI Chairman to present the case for anti-corruption in business when Transparency International was launched in Indonesia. Similarly, the Forum for Corporate Governance in Indonesia (FCGI) has described UI as 'a model company', and the NGO MTI invited UI to a seminar to talk about how the private sector can fight corruption. In the future, UI's commitment to anti-corruption initiatives within the wider business community might be measured by the promotion of this agenda in the Indonesian Chamber of Commerce.

Key insights: UI's wider impact in the community

Oxfam and Unilever agree that the greatest potential for achieving impacts that benefit people living in poverty lies within UI's mainstream operations and value chain, which have been the primary focus of this research project. Nonetheless, voluntary community involvement can also provide a positive interaction with society, bringing benefits not only to communities, but directly and indirectly to the business itself.

UI's approach to voluntary engagement has changed over time, moving away from traditional forms of philanthropic giving and donations. Increasingly, the company links its own knowledge and skills base with its voluntary efforts. For example, UI supports a programme for Indonesians who have no established business networks or connections, giving them the opportunity to become entrepreneurs. Similarly, UI supports another programme – run jointly with the Indonesian government – which provides SME start-ups with market access, technical skills, and access to finance. Scaled up with the support of government, CSOs, and the wider business community, programmes like these can enable people living in poverty to build their skill levels and participate more profitably in the formal economy.

UI's influence on the business sector and government was not explored in depth by this research project. UI is in a strong position to set a positive example in these areas, and points to the success of its long-term relations with its business partnerships, conducted in line with its business principles, as an indicator of good practice. The challenge lies in identifying more measurable ways of assessing company performance in this area, for the benefit not only of the business community, but also for the Indonesian people more generally who comprise its market.

UI has been successful in improving the capacity of its business partners and carrying out a series of activities that benefit communities in the areas in which it operates and beyond. It is important to learn how these practices position companies like UI in the overall development of the country.

7 Conclusions

Unilever and Oxfam have worked together on this project since January 2004. The work was ambitious, challenging, and very time-consuming. The goal was to question assumptions about foreign direct investment and multinational companies, and their impacts on poverty. This project was made possible through the efforts of each organisation to learn from the other: for Oxfam to increase its understanding of how companies work, and for Unilever to understand the fundamental assumptions and concerns of civil-society organisations. The research and analysis covered a lot of ground. The project was intended to bring together very different world-views, as well as different approaches to research and analysis.

For both organisations there are risks arising from their engagement in this project. Unilever opened its doors to Oxfam, and Oxfam agreed to observe conditions of confidentiality. Both risk criticisms from partner organisations and colleagues who are sceptical about the potential role of MNCs to contribute to development that benefits people living in poverty, or about the role of CSOs in demonstrating that companies can contribute to pro-poor development while also maintaining financially viable business strategies.

Both organisations have learned a tremendous amount in this process. Some of their lessons have been similar, and some have been quite different. The learning, however, would not have occurred without intensive and often difficult debate, which contributed to constructive discussion and analysis. In the end, both organisations have found common ground – considerably more than they had expected to find. Despite their very different world-views, they have built trust to enable them to work as partners throughout this research project.

This concluding chapter contains four sections. The first two present the lessons learned from the project by Oxfam and Unilever respectively, including insights arising from the research content and insights arising from the project process and partnership. The third section contains a selection of key comments and issues raised by members of the external reference group who read a draft of the report. The final section indicates areas for further research, and some next steps for both Oxfam and Unilever.

Content: lessons learned from the research project

Oxfam: lessons learned from the research

1   Many companies still see their purpose as profit maximisation, but we have learned from Unilever that in many cases business decisions rarely amount to a strictly profit-based calculation. The notion that 'the business of business is business' is outdated, and there are huge opportunities for civil society to engage with companies to explore how they might use their influence to raise performance standards, distribute resources, share knowledge, and innovate for the common good.

2   We also learned that our analysis needs to be more alert to the differences between multinational companies. At every point in its value chain, UI's business is highly dependent on Indonesians: as producers, suppliers, employees, contract workers, distributors, retailers, and consumers. UI's business decisions and choices reflect the embedded nature of its operations, favouring a long-term approach to optimising opportunities for business success, and an emphasis on the development of skills and industry within the wider Indonesian economy. As such, UI is very different from some of the traditional targets of CSO campaigning, such as extractive or export-processing industries. These differences have important implications for an understanding of UI's poverty footprint; moreover, an appreciation of them can help us to understand why and how a company like UI might be motivated to study and improve its poverty impacts. Our findings suggest that highly embedded MNCs and large domestic companies might in future provide a focus for useful work on private-sector poverty impacts and poverty-reduction strategies.

3   This project also challenged our assumption that the growth of an MNC in a domestic market necessarily means a parallel shrinking of domestic companies. The research was not adequate to support definitive conclusions on this key area of debate. However, it appears that during the period under review competing domestic industries had expanded rather than contracted — although there could be many reasons for this.

4   While there is an increasing number of corporate social responsibility measures in place, there is nothing that allows companies to conduct a systematic assessment of their positive and negative contributions to poverty reduction throughout the value chain. This project has increased our understanding of UI's poverty footprint in Indonesia. It also provides the company with some insights into how they can increase their overall contribution to poverty reduction and perhaps eventually develop a 'pro-poor policy'. This is a powerful concept, which may be useful for engagement with other companies.

5   We have seen how decisions that are pro-business can also be pro-poor. UI's response to the financial crisis in 1997–98 appears to be largely a 'win–win' approach. It was good for business, because it expanded UI's

market base; but it was also pro-poor, because the increased forward and backward linkages meant that UI's activities protected jobs at a time when many companies were closing their operations. Companies that take a longer-term view of their in-country operations have greater potential to contribute to poverty reduction, and may also gain market share.

6   In its campaigns and programmes, Oxfam has learned about and drawn attention to the risks of 'precarious employment' for individuals, families, societies, and even employers. Precarious employment is often the result of the twin trends of increased outsourcing and use of contract workers on company premises. In this project, Oxfam learned how companies may perceive these trends as inevitable and necessary, and an important part of their core business strategy. A challenge for Oxfam is how to acknowledge the trend but suggest feasible alternatives that avoid its often negative consequences.

7   We have gained a better understanding of the potential of distribution chains to generate employment and income. Our research found that for every direct employee there were many more jobs in distribution chains. For NGOs currently focusing their efforts on improving conditions for producers and other workers within *supply* chains, the research shows that it may also be valuable to analyse MNC policies towards the *distribution and retail* aspect of their value chains.

8   However, as a result of this project, it became clearer that participation in value chains alone does not guarantee improvements in the living conditions of poor people. This reinforced our belief that for value chains to work for poor people, there need to be other social institutions and resources in place, such as credit and saving schemes, marketing associations, and insurance schemes, as well as diversification of income streams, to avoid dependency on any single company or market.

9   We also learned how difficult it is to arrive at a specific definition of what constitutes 'fair practice' by companies. This issue is not as clearly defined as we would like it to be. For example, despite international definitions of 'a living wage' and how to calculate it, and despite the national definition of a legal minimum wage, it remains difficult to judge the appropriateness of MNC wage levels within a given context. For example, how much above the legally required minimum wage is it appropriate for an MNC to pay? And to what extent can the same policies be encouraged for an MNC's suppliers and contractors? Similarly we debated, but did not resolve, the concept of a 'fair price' and the question of how much expenditure on advertising is appropriate as a proportion of consumer prices.

10   MNCs like Unilever are often challenged to encourage better working conditions in the national economy through their value-chain contracts with other companies. During this project, Oxfam explored with UI the realities and complexities faced by a large company in attempting to raise the standards of other companies within its value chain. The ability

of UI to demand better working conditions within its value chain depends partly on the level of competition between companies in the chain, and partly on the national legal framework within which business must operate. In addition, it is influenced by the culture of business in Indonesia, which emphasises relationships and dialogue over contract-driven demand.

11 The greatest challenge posed by this project was to understand and agree on the impact of marketing practices on people living in poverty. Both Unilever and Oxfam entered these discussions with extremely entrenched views. Each assumed that differences of opinion could be resolved with objective data, but in the end we had to agree that there were some fundamental differences in our interpretation, and we would have to 'agree to disagree'. It was a challenge for Oxfam to disregard value-based issues that to us represent the interests of poor consumers, and instead focus our analysis on the objective factors that could be shown to have an impact on poverty.

Unilever: lessons learned from the research

1 The primary lesson for us is the insight that we gained into the extent of the widespread 'job' multiplier in UI's total value chain. While the FTE calculations in this report are admittedly estimates, the findings nonetheless point to the potential use of value-chain policies as a tool in sustainable poverty reduction. As such it will be useful to share the insights of the FMCG value-chain multiplier, and the opportunities that it offers, with all those concerned with poverty-reduction strategies.

2 The spread of value-adding activity throughout the value chain creates a broad tax base. A predictable tax base is essential for the development of the formal economy on which the government can build, and finance, its social and environmental programmes. This report addresses only the direct taxes paid by UI to the Indonesian government. Further research could explore the scale of taxes paid by the many players involved in an FMCG value chain, including both companies and individual workers.

3 FMCG value chains can offer poor people an opportunity to gain basic skills within a structured learning environment and earn incremental, regular income. Although imperfect, these opportunities in turn may be the first steps towards accumulating assets, increasing independence, and improving quality of life. Oxfam has pointed out that for poor people who participate in FMCG value chains there may be negative impacts, such as poor working terms and conditions, or debt and financing difficulties. These are areas that need particular care and attention. Government, businesses, and CSOs can each play a part in helping to gain the best outcomes for poor people.

4 However carefully standards are designed and implemented, there is always room for improvement. The scrutiny of UI's relationship with low-income consumers, and its contractor-review processes, suggested

ways in which the company could improve its pro-poor impacts. Specifically, the company will look at opportunities for developing a better understanding of low-income consumers in the light of the points raised by Oxfam. Through the contract-review process, UI will check to ensure that contractors in the value chain are meeting their commitments to workplace policies and standards, in particular on gender issues, especially in terms of the effects of their policies and standards on women.

5   Even where there is a shared appreciation of the benefits of an alternative supply chain, as in the black-soybean project, it is recognised that there are constraints and limitations on the viability of the model, and doubts about whether the model itself represents the answer to the problems of poor farmers. Where it can, Unilever will continue to work with a wide range of partners, including NGOs, to seek better, sustainable practices to reduce negative social and environmental impacts in the production of the agricultural crops that it purchases.

6   A persistent focus on the position of the individual living in poverty – whether man, woman, or child – is essential for developing sustainable poverty-reduction strategies. Oxfam held the line on this matter throughout the project, and the Unilever team acknowledged its importance. For a company like UI which interacts with people living in poverty, this mindset and the feedback that it creates offer an opportunity to increase the positive impacts of its activities and reduce the negative impacts. It also indicates that while a company has an important 'product-delivering, wealth-creating, skills-transferring' role, it is only one participant alongside other businesses, governments, international institutions, and CSOs in the drive for sustainable poverty reduction. For optimum impact, a concerted effort is required.

7   It was disappointing not to have had more time to explore the role of UI in the marketplace, the pricing and availability of its products, the purpose of brands, and issues involved in advertising. The sheer momentum of change taking place, not only in the marketplace but in Indonesian society in general, makes it very difficult to separate individual strands of cause and effect. In UI's experience, consumers are keenly aware of value for money and quality, and are ready to reject any brand that fails to meet their increasingly sophisticated expectations.

Process and partnership: lessons learned from working together

It was clear from the outset, and certainly reinforced by this work, that no single actor will be able to understand fully – much less resolve – the issues raised in this report. That being said, partnerships are not easy to develop and are even harder to maintain over time. Within this project, it has been particularly difficult to reach joint agreement on the text. The lessons learned by Oxfam and Unilever are listed separately below, even though many are overlapping. The nuances of the lessons learned reflect each organisation's particular values and levels of understanding of the issues.

Oxfam: lessons learned from the partnership

1   This project represented a big step for Oxfam in its work with the private sector. Although we have studied companies and whole sectors in the past, we have never gone so far in exploring the motivations, trade-offs, and choices that companies make in their operations. The insights into the private sector that we have gained from this project will equip us for more powerful engagement in the future.

2   Could Oxfam have done this project on its own? We could not have assessed UI's value chain without the help of UI staff and our review of their internal documents. Any analysis that we could have done by ourselves would have been incomplete and superficial. We now have a much deeper understanding of UI's business operations and the full range of its interactions in Indonesia. Without this partnership we would have probably reached some wrong conclusions. This experience has reinforced for us the role that engagement can play in understanding and then influencing a company's strategy.

3   At the outset, we expected to focus most of our energy on the research. In the end, most was focused on analysing and interpreting the data, and expressing the points of agreement and disagreement in this joint report. We were often frustrated by difficult negotiations over language, but we came to realise that negotiating a common text forced us to understand each other in a way that would have been impossible if we had written separate documents. The real learning came through these Oxfam–Unilever dialogues.

4   Once we started the analysis, it became apparent that the modest research effort undertaken to support this project would not provide the data needed to answer the initial questions that we had wanted to answer. We needed more time for research, and ideally we should have included follow-up research to fill gaps that emerged in our data. Having several types of evidence – Unilever's data, facts from external researchers, and data that we gathered for ourselves through on-site interviews with research teams – proved to be very useful. We would probably do more of the latter if we were to engage in a similar project – particularly to strengthen the gender analysis, because gender-related

statistics rarely appeared in the official or corporate data that we analysed.

5 At the outset, we assumed that the research would provide a factual basis for understanding core dilemmas posed by the private sector's impact on people living in poverty. In practice, we found that there were often very significant differences in interpretation of the same set of objective data. While the research provided some important grounding, we realised that many of the issues that are debated between civil-society organisations and the private sector are defined by prior assumptions, core values, and beliefs. These cannot necessarily be resolved by gathering evidence, although evidence helps to identify areas of agreement and to understand areas of disagreement. This experience points to a very different approach in corporate social responsibility work, one which goes beyond data collection to a more intensive and rigorous dialogue, ideally as a step towards action.

6 During the project Oxfam and Unilever came to realise that, despite their very different missions and goals, they share a commitment to contributing to poverty reduction and development. The greatest differences were determined by our expectations of what companies can and cannot be expected to contribute to poverty reduction, the promotion of social and economic rights, and national development. By the end of the project, we were much closer to understanding these limitations and opportunities.

7 We learned a huge amount about analysing value chains, and we discovered that this is a very powerful tool for understanding a company's range of impacts on people living in poverty. Having access to company data was key to developing this picture, and in this respect UI's willingness to share information with us was indispensable. There is much to be done to develop a robust methodology for value-chain analysis, and we hope that other Unilever operations and other companies will make their data available and share in this analysis.

8 Our process was flawed in failing to create sufficient opportunities for stakeholder input, learning, and reflection. Although we attempted to establish a reference group, the difficulties of finding common ground between Unilever and Oxfam meant that we were hesitant to open up the draft text for further comment. We know that we will have disappointed some of our partners in Indonesia for not making this possible, and we know that the result is poorer for having failed in this respect. We hope that we will be able to establish a dialogue with stakeholders in the next stage of this work.

9 The brief period of research on which the project depended provided a mere 'snapshot', a moment in the lives of those interviewed. Given the vulnerability of the poorest people in the value chain, their interactions with a company can change dramatically in a short time. We could have learned more by checking back one year later to see whether the initial findings were still relevant, which would have helped us to develop a picture of the trends that underlie the data.

10 Finally, we have learned about the challenges of sharing learning within large organisations. The experience has been significant for the people involved, but we are aware that follow-up is essential if the lessons learned are to become embedded in policy and practice. We hope that we will find ways to integrate this learning by continuing dialogue, both internally and externally, to achieve an even better understanding of these issues.

Unilever: lessons learned from the partnership

1   The project design as set out in the MOU provided a robust framework within which to manage this complex project. In particular, defining the statement of intent gave clarity to our purpose; agreeing the 'rules of engagement' for the project team enabled open sharing of information; the third-party author introduced a fresh perspective during intense discussions; and the reference group and dispute-resolution process (although the latter was never invoked) eased pressure, because we knew that we had a way to manage irreconcilable differences if they arose.

2   However, we over-estimated the scope of a third-party author to resolve contested issues, and the management of the dialogue process could have been strengthened. These shortcomings pushed the project team to work through each issue together. This dramatically increased the project timescale. However, it also significantly increased the learning, as we worked together (where possible) towards a common under-standing. But this common understanding, when achieved, is difficult to communicate quickly and easily to other, more sceptical, non-team members.

3   We knew this would be a very big project and we tried to address the scale and complexity of the research by limiting it to the operations of UI. But there was still a large amount of data to analyse and understand. This fact contributed to the project's over-run.

4   Management data, in the form of Key Performance Indicators (KPIs), are of limited value when the processes and systems whose performance they are used to indicate are not in themselves understood. For example, LTA (Lost Time Accident) figures are only the ultimate statistic of a whole body of management processes and values. In Unilever/UI the management of health and safety is only one aspect of a broader management philosophy of TPM (Total Productive Manufacturing). Achieving a common understanding of management knowledge took considerably longer than had been expected, but was essential to explaining why UI managers placed confidence in their ways of working, and why the performance data presented were both robust and important.

5   Unilever publishes an annual global social report, based on data and information collected from its businesses around the world. In addition, some of our local operating companies publish summaries of their own

social performance for local audiences. This project was the first time we had worked closely with an NGO to analyse our social and economic impacts in a particular country. The independent research gave us new insights and information in a number of areas, including new perspectives and ways of looking at social issues. Information resulting from such research may be significantly different in emphasis and quality from that generated by our business-management and self-assessment systems. From our work over many years with environmental NGOs, we have recognised the importance of taking into account a range of views which through direct constructive engagement may result in new insights into how to move forward. This project was a valuable example of direct engagement on a very wide range of social and economic issues.

6 Once the field work was completed, much of the remaining work was essentially desk research, analysis, and writing. Still, the human interaction during the key project-team meetings was critical to developing levels of trust and confidence, which in turn enabled us to probe deep-seated preconceptions on both sides, and explore sometimes painful perceptions of the reality of business operations. Without these face-to-face sessions, the value of the project and the final product would have been diminished.

7 The most productive way to take this data-rich research report forward will be in interactive, face-to-face learning workshops, approached in a spirit of transparent, open-minded enquiry, and willingness to learn.

Feedback from the external reference group

Feedback from our external reference group on a well-developed draft of this report helped us to shape the final version, in particular by identifying areas where restructuring or more explanation would clarify our key messages. Specific questions and suggestions from the reference group included the following:

- Clearly set out Oxfam's and Unilever's motivations for engaging in the project. Be clear that this was a 'learning project'.
- The report should ask 'What is the "role" of business in tackling poverty?' Clarify the question of motivation for pro-poor decisions or actions by a company. What is it reasonable to ask companies to do?
- Present the dilemmas, trade-offs, and complexities that companies face in trying to create pro-poor impacts.
- Be explicit on the different opinions and the different learnings of Oxfam and Unilever from this project.
- Recognise that the role of the government and other externalities and the private sector are not fully explored in this report.
- More gender analysis would strengthen the report.
- Explore other raw-material supply chains, in addition to the Kecap Bango chain.

- Be more explicit about the importance, and the business case for, corporate philanthropic activities in addressing social issues.

- Acknowledge the implications of this report for others, especially other companies.

- Recognise the scale of this project: no one company or NGO can make an impact on its own. Partnerships and buy-in from a range of stakeholders are essential.

- Clarify the research process undertaken by this project.

- Take care that the report does not sound like a corporate brochure; avoid 'PR speak'.

The project team appreciated the time and attention that the reference group gave to providing feedback on the draft report. The team was especially grateful for the detailed comments and suggestions, which were incorporated wherever possible when finalising the report. Responsibility for the report and its conclusions remains with the project team.

The way forward

While this research offers a data-rich study, it is still incomplete. Building on these initial findings will require broader participation and would benefit from drawing on some of the research methodologies currently being developed by leading academics in the field of corporate social responsibility, to support the partnering and learning process. Of the substantive questions that remain, we have identified several key questions for future research:

- The general findings of this research for the generation of employment and revenue along the value chain were surprising. Do they hold for other companies in the FMCG industry? What does this mean for the design of pro-poor development strategies?

- This research suggests that there are likely to be differences of opinion over what are reasonable performance expectations within different sectors. Additional research that would allow side-by-side comparisons of the performance of oil and gas companies, mining companies, export-led manufacturers, and banks might suggest the types of trade-off that occur when governments encourage one type of FDI over others.

- It is clear from this work that MNCs like UI can have impacts on local economies by sharing good-practice standards. What are the best ways for a company to extend its policies and practices through the value chain?

- This work focused almost exclusively on the private sector. What can and should government be encouraged to do to promote an enabling environment for private-sector investment that supports pro-poor development?

- The data available for this study were insufficient to allow us to draw strong conclusions about the gender-differentiated impacts of the changing systems of labour use on the supply and retail sides of the value chain.

- Pursuing research from a people-centred perspective, where people living in poverty are the starting point and their views are fully reflected, is an obvious priority for a follow-up research project.

- Finally, we found discussions about the impact of advertising and marketing practices on poverty to be particularly challenging. This is a key issue from the perspectives of both poverty and business viability. It would be good to understand these relationships better.

During the course of the project, Unilever's project team discussed the management of the exercise, its contents, and its conclusions with colleagues in different roles within UI and the wider business. The Unilever project team has worked to create and maintain the space in which lessons could be jointly learned. On publication, the report will be disseminated within Unilever as part of the company's programme to increase management's understanding of Unilever's social impacts, a process which the project team believes will lead to further learning.

Oxfam, too, will distribute this report broadly to its partners and colleagues, to show how different approaches to partnership and research and analysis yield different insights and strategies. This research has developed Oxfam's understanding of how businesses operate, and where and how to influence business behaviour. Oxfam hopes to continue working with Unilever to interpret and implement the findings of this research, and expects to begin to develop similar initiatives with other companies as well.

In crossing boundaries and working together, the project team aimed to bring a new perspective to the links between multinational business activities and poverty reduction. We hope this report will be a useful and encouraging resource for anyone concerned about this subject – including people in other businesses, CSOs, governments, international agencies, and universities, and the many individuals who, like us, struggle with these complex and challenging issues.

Notes

1   'Oxfam' in this report refers to Oxfam GB and Novib Oxfam Netherlands, two of twelve members of Oxfam International.

2   The Millennium and Johannesburg Declarations (2000, 2002) place poverty eradication at the centre of global strategies for sustainable development.

3   In this report, the term 'civil-society organisation' (CSO) refers to not-for-profit organisations which are not part of any State or government structure. It includes primarily non-government organisations, trade unions, religious groups, independent media, and other networks or civic organisations.

4   See www.unilever.com, www.oxfam.org, www.novib.nl

5   In fact, there are hundreds of relationships in each of dozens of different value chains; they are referred to in this report as 'the value chain' for the sake of simplicity.

6   Unilever is participating in the Roundtable on Sustainable Palm Oil, which is developing standards for plantation establishment as well as better practices to reduce the industry's negative social and environmental impacts. Similarly, Unilever has developed extensive guidelines on better management practices (BMPs) for tea production, and it participates in the Ethical Tea Partnership. (See Box 6.)

7   This is a standard measure used by the World Bank, UN, and others, which takes into account different costs of goods and services to calculate 'Purchasing Power Parity', thus allowing comparisons across countries.

8   Hereafter this is referred to as 'the minimum wage'.

9   The parent company does purchase raw and processed materials for export.

10   This calculation is based on company research showing that 95 per cent of all Indonesians buy UI products, and that the income of just over half of all Indonesians falls below the international poverty line of $2 per day.

11   Parastatals are companies that are owned wholly or partly by the government.

12   Price-to-earnings ratio is the price of a stock divided by its earnings. It provides an indication of investors' expectations of future profits.

13   Unilever policy forbids operating companies to use funds to speculate on currencies, interest rates, and financial markets.

14   Oxfam communication with staff of FPBN (Forum Pendamping Buruh, the National Forum of Labour Rights NGOs).

15   UI does not hold data on skill levels of its contract workers; but of those interviewed for this research, one-fifth were skilled workers.

16   Internal management data.

17   Unilever, CSR Review 2000.

18   See Oxfam International, *Trading Away Our Rights*, 2000, pp. 17-21; Cisadane Labour Committee (2003), 'Initial Findings of Investigation by the Cisadane Labour Committee into the Contract Work System', unpublished report, Indonesia; Sarah Gardner, 'Women in trade unions', *Inside Indonesia*, No. 76, October–December, 2003.

19   Indonesian Labour Law no. 13/2003, chapters 56, 59, 64, 65.

20   Unless otherwise specified, all quantitative data in this section come from UI internal management reports.

21   For example, the unplanned purchase of small office equipment or spare parts for emergency use.

22   This is based on research undertaken for this report.

23   This increased to Rp 750 million in 2004. Data provided by Pak Achmad Zubaidi from PT Sorini.

24   This is based on research undertaken for this report.

25   The primary producers in UI's supply chain include small-scale farmers and agricultural workers employed on farms and plantations. This research focuses on small-scale farmers, not on plantation workers or farm labourers. The conclusions in this report about poverty impacts for small-scale farmers within the supply chain do not necessarily hold true for these other types of poor agricultural worker.

26   All data in this paragraph are from UI internal management reports.

27   The Unilever purchasing figures for palm oil and tea were provided by Unilever. The market-share estimates were calculated by the report author, using data published by FAO STAT.

28   AC Nielsen survey, 2004.

29   This was estimated from information in UI management reports and the research team.

30   The figures in Figure 6 are based on actual or best-estimate data available during the preparation of this report. Some of the information was generated through the background research, some was provided directly by UI, and some data were estimated on the basis of information obtained from UI and independent sources. The estimates are realistic, and probably conservative, but are not complete and should be used for indicative purposes only.

31   For more information on this topic, see recent AccountAbility / BSR reports at www.economicfootprint.org

32   Professor C.K. Prahalad's book, *The Fortune at the Bottom of the Pyramid*, is arguably the best known of a growing number of publications focusing on marketing to poor consumers as an opportunity and growth area for companies.

33   Association of Cosmetic Companies. Data on size of companies and market share were not available.

34   UI Annual Report 2002.

35   Figures based on one visit to a Jakarta *warung* by Oxfam in 2004.

36   UI internal CSR reports, 2002.

37   Internal CSR records, 2003.

38   Conversation with Tonny Pranatadjaja, Unilever Indonesia.

References and sources

Antos, Jim n.d. Global Equity Research/Unilever Indonesia. Available at www.ubswarburg.com/researchweb

Asian Labour News (2004) *Review – State concerns: unemployment angst*, Laksamana, 18 January 2004

Asiaweek (2001) *Asiaweek 1000: The region's largest companies*, 9 November 2001, Time Inc. Available at www.asiaweek.com

Biro Pusat Statistik SAKERNAS: *Indonesia National Labour Force Survey, 1996, 1999, 2000, and 2000*, Jakarta: BPS

CLSA (2001) *Saints and Sinners—Who's Got Religion? Corporate Governance in Emerging Markets*, Corporate Governance Watch, Hong Kong: CLSA

Coalition of Dutch CSO & Trade Unions (2003) *CSR Frame of Reference*, The Netherlands: MVO-Platform

Economist Intelligence Unit (2003) *Indonesia Country Forecast*, London: Economist Intelligence Unit

Friedrich Ebert Stiftung (2004) *Country Analysis Indonesia*, 13 December 2004

Gadjah Mada University Team (2004) 'Black Soybean Seed Development', Yogyakarta: Gadjah Mada University

Gardner, Sarah (2003) 'Women in trade unions', *Inside Indonesia* 76 (Oct/Dec), Melbourne: Indonesia Resources and Information Programme Incorporated

Goodman, D. and M. Watts (eds.) (1997) *Globalizing Food: Agrarian Questions and Global Restructuring,* New York: Routledge

IMD (2001) *World Competitiveness Yearbook 2001*, Geneva: IMD

IMF (2004) *International Financial Statistics Yearbook 2004,* Washington DC: IMF

International Labour Organization (ILO) (1999) 'Towards Gender Equality in the World of Work in Asia and the Pacific', Technical Report for discussion at the Asian Regional Consultation on the Follow-up to the Fourth World Conference on Women. Manila, 6–8 October 1999, Bangkok: ILO Regional Office for Asia and the Pacific

Ionescu-Somers, Aileen (2001) 'Unilever Indonesia: Linking Business Strategy To Job Creation', paper prepared under the supervision of Professor Ulrich Steger, International Institute for Management Development, Lausanne, Switzerland

Prahalad, C.K. (2004) *The Fortune at the Bottom of the Pyramid*, University of Pennsylvania, Wharton School of Publishing

SMERU Research Institute (2001) *Wage and Employment Effects of Minimum Wage Policy in the Indonesian Urban Labor Market*, Indonesia: SMERU Research Institute

State Gazette of the Republic of Indonesia (2003) *Act of the Republic of Indonesia Number 13 concerning Manpower*, unofficial translation, Government of Indonesia

Tambusai, M. (2004) 'New labor law causes workers more distress', *The Jakarta Post,* 26 August

UNCTAD (2003) *Trade and Development Report 2003*

Unilever Indonesia (2002) *The Journey to Excellence,* Annual Report, Jakarta, Indonesia

Unilever Indonesia (2003) *Grow People for Growth,* Annual Report, Jakarta, Indonesia

Unilever Indonesia (2003) 'Company Baseline (2002) Data', from the Corporate Social Responsibility Self-Assessment Project

Unilever Indonesia (2004) 'Presentation to CSR and Oxfam visitors: Country and Company Update', Jakarta, Indonesia

Unilever International (2002) *Listening, Learning, Making Progress*, Social Review, London

Unilever International (2003) *Listening, Learning, Update on Progress,* Summary Social Review, London

World Bank Indonesia (2003) *CGI Brief: Beyond Macro-economic Stability*, p. 53, Jakarta, December 2003

World Business Council for Sustainable Development (2004) *Doing Business with the Poor,* Field Guide, Geneva: WBCSD

United Nations Development Programme (2004)*Human Development Report 2004*, 'Cultural Liberty in Today's Diverse World', New York: UNDP

Widianto, Bambang (2003) 'Employment Creation and Labor Market Flexibility', National Development Planning Agency, Jakarta: BAPPENAS

Appendix 1: The project team

Project board

Becky Buell, Head of Programme Policy, Campaigns and Policy Division, Oxfam GB

Mandy Cormack, Unilever

Michelle Dow, The Corporate Citizenship Company

Heather Grady, Global Adviser on Rights and Institutional Accountability, Oxfam GB

Andrew Kinmont, Unilever

David Logan, The Corporate Citizenship Company

Tonny Pranatadjaja, Unilever Indonesia

Retno Winahyu, Project Manager, Oxfam/Unilever Joint Research Project, Oxfam GB

Other Unilever team members

Okty Damayanti, Unilever Indonesia

Rachmat Hidayat, Unilever Indonesia

Muhammad Saleh, Unilever Indonesia

Anne Weir, Unilever

Other Oxfam team members

Alison Beaumont, Designer, Campaigns and Policy Division, Oxfam GB

Lea Borkenhagen, Livelihoods Programme Development Manager, Campaigns and Policy Division, Oxfam GB

Anna Coryndon, Managing Editor, Campaigns and Policy Division, Oxfam GB

Sumi Dhanarajan, Private Sector Adviser, Campaigns and Policy Division, Oxfam GB

Kate Kilpatrick, Global Adviser, Campaigns and Policy Division, Oxfam GB

Yanty Lacsana, Deputy Country Programme Manager, Indonesia, Oxfam GB

David Macdonald, Country Programme Manager, Indonesia, Oxfam GB

Purnama Adil Marata, Labour Programme Officer, Indonesia, Oxfam GB

Kate Raworth, Research and Policy Adviser, Campaigns and Policy Division, Oxfam GB

Catherine Robinson, Editor, Oxfam Publishing, Campaigns and Policy Division, Oxfam GB

Sophia Tickell, Policy Adviser, Oxfam GB

Liesbeth Unger, Adviser on Corporate Social Responsibility for East Asia, Novib Oxfam Netherlands

Johan Verburg, Adviser on Corporate Social Responsibility, Novib Oxfam Netherlands

Researchers

T. Hani Handoko

A. Prasetyantoko

B.M. Purwanto

Maria Ratnaningsih

Principal author

Jason Clay, World Wildlife Fund for Nature, with input from Amar Inamdar, Synergy

Reference group

Emy Ardjakusuma, Director General of Domestic Trade, Department of Industry and Trade, Indonesia

Mas Daniri, Chairman, National Committee on Governance, Indonesia

Robert Davies, The Prince of Wales International Business Leaders Forum, UK

John Humphrey, Institute of Development, Sussex University, UK

Gilbert Lenssen, European Academy of Business in Society, Brussels, Belgium

Satish Mishra, UNSFIR, Indonesia

Bagus Muharyo, Social Institute Foundation, Indonesia

Januar Nugroho, formerly Business Watch Indonesia

Suzanne Siskel, Ford Foundation, Indonesia

Muhamad Suhud, International NGO Forum on Indonesian Development, Indonesia

Bondan Winarno, Ex-Editor in Chief, Suara Pembaharuan, Indonesia

Appendix 2: UI product list, 2003

Personal-care products

Skin care

Dove Bar

Dove Facial Foam

Citra Beauty Lotion Mangir *

Citra White Lotion Bangkoang *

Citra Refreshing Milk Cleanser (anti-acne)

Citra Refreshing Milk Cleanser (white)

Vaseline Intensive Care Lotion

Pond's White Beauty Skin Lightening (Lotion & Cream)

Pond's White Beauty Shake and Clean

Pond's White Beauty Cleansing Milk

Pond's White Beauty Face Toner

Pond's Complete Whitening Care

Pond's Perfect Care Shake & Clean

Pond's Anti Bacterial Facial

Pond's White Beauty Facial Foam

* also in sachet

Deodorant

Rexona Roll-On

Axe Body Spray

Rexona Deodorant Stick

Axe Antiperspirant Stick

Rexona Antiperspirant Stick

Toothpaste

Close-Up Gel

Close-Up Eucalyptus Mint

Close-Up Crystal

Pepsodent Plus Whitening

Pepsodent Gigi Susu

Pepsodent Herbal

Pepsodent Junior

Pepsodent Triple Action

Pepsodent Toothbrush

Hair care

Sunsilk Shampoo*

Lifebuoy Shampoo*

Clear Shampoo*

Brisk Hair Cream

* also in sachet

Tissues

Kleenex Bag

Trentis Bag

Kleenex — Facial Box

Scott — Facial Box

Trentis Tissue — Facial Box

Kleenex Tissue — Facial Handkerchief

Trentis Facial Handkerchief

Kleenex Facial Refill

Scott Facial Refill

Trentis Napkin

Baby diapers

Huggies Dry Comfort

Huggies Dry

Feminine care

Kotex Mainstream

Kotex Regular

Kotex Special Package

Personal wash

Lux Toilet Soap

Lifebuoy Toilet Soap

Lux Beauty

Lux Beauty Shower

Lifebuoy Body Wash

Halo Hand Wash Liquid

Household products

Dishwash

Sunlight Cream

Sunlight Scourer

Vim Scourer

Sunlight Liquid

Fabric softeners

Molto Trika

Molto Pewangi

Molto Softener

Molto Refresh

Fabric wash

Omo — Sunlight Hard Soap

Rinso Excel

Rinso Anti Noda*

Rinso Warna*

Surf Powder*

Rinsomatic

* also in sachet

Mosquito coil

Domestos Nomos

Household cleaner

Super Pell

Vixal Porcelain Cleaner

Dometos Trisol

Domestos Wipol

Kiff Glass Cleaner

CIF Furnish Furniture

Food products

Beverages

Lipton Yellow Label Tea Bags

Sariwangi Tea Bags & sachet

Lipton Ice Tea Can

Lipton Ice Tea Tetra

Snack

Taro

Seasoning

Royco Flour

Bango Kecap in bottle & refill pouch

Royco Fds Powder in sachet.

Margarine

Blue Band Margarine in tin, tube, and sachet

Ice-cream products (Walls)

Paddle Pop

Cornetto

Feast

Magnum

Popular

Rocket

Viennetta

Other products

Pepsodent Delicio